Death of a Spouse

—— My Journey ——

A Memoir by
Erwin Parent

BALBOA.
PRESS
A DIVISION OF HAY HOUSE

Balboa Press books may be ordered through booksellers or by contacting:

Balboa Press
A Division of Hay House
1663 Liberty Drive
Bloomington, IN 47403
www.balboapress.com
1 (877) 407-4847

Print information available on the last page.

ISBN: 978-1-5043-6994-7 (sc)
ISBN: 978-1-5043-6995-4 (e)

Balboa Press rev. date: 01/17/2017

DEDICATION

I dedicate this book posthumously to the two loves of my life: Virginia Allen Parent and Rosanna Gibson Parent

CONTENTS

ACKNOWLEDGEMENTS

I want to thank my sister Jan and her husband Ted Kibby for standing by me during many of the events in this Memoir

Thanks to my son Geoff and his wife Danielle for supporting me. I had a good balance of time alone to write and time to spend with the grandkids

Thanks to my son Gregory who lived through both of these events and has been supportive in many ways.

Thanks to my son Gary and his wife Eunice. You have been a huge help.

The Family Hospice Care - The service used in Desert Hot Springs CA for Rosanna

Rev. Carolyn A. Grzecki - for sharing her firsthand experience regarding Grief Counseling

Modesto Writers Group – Thanks for all your help, I could not have done this without you. All your valuable input and support will not be forgotten

INTRODUCTION

This is a love story, in fact two love stories. I am so fortunate to have had two wonderful women in my life.

This is my first attempt at writing. I have no literary background. During my career in Information Technology as a Technical Writer I would produce User Guides and Procedure Manuals.

Losing a loved one is a terrible experience. I don't believe anyone can write a book on how everyone should handle the loss. The experience is so unique and there are so many variables such as individual beliefs and backgrounds. I was married twice. Today marriage may not be the norm. So when I mention spouse it can be husband or wife. It also could be significant other or long-time partner. From here on I will use the term "your loved one" to include all.

I was married first, to Virginia Allen, a marriage that lasted 35 years. Virginia died of Ovarian Cancer 75 days after it was diagnosed. I then fell in love again at age 57, and married Rosanna Gibson. This marriage lasted 17 years. She too died of Ovarian Cancer 45 days after it was diagnosed. They both died in the month of September, both on a Sunday. I take the marriage vows sacred and am so grateful to have had them both in my life. I added another vow: that they would not die among strangers. I was able to keep them both at home and was alone with them in the end. I cherish those final moments with them both and would not want it any other way.

I cannot just share the loss of each one without including how we met and about our lives together as a couple.

So I will write 3 chapters on each:
    Meeting, Marrying and Losing Virginia
    Meeting, Marrying and Losing Rosanna

Two more chapters will conclude my thoughts
    Harvesting the Seeds Sown as a Couple
    Collection of Dreams, Experiences and Events after both died

I will also share how I was able to turn negatives into positives and include these in a summary at the end of each chapter offering you some thoughts and advice.

After the death of Virginia, I was totally lost. I kept to myself and would try to write something to help me overcome this terrible event. I always loved poetry. Coming from New England my favorite was Robert Frost, he had such simplicity about him. I was brought up in Christian Science. The Founder, Mary Baker Eddy also wrote poetry. Several of her poems were set to music and are in the church hymnal today.

As I started jotting down notes I found I was writing lines of poetry. This seemed a comfortable way to document my thoughts. This was the first time I ever attempted to write verse. As I wrote, I was not concentrating on the correctness of the meter or type of verse. It just flowed from my thought. Many are two-line rhyming verses which I still use today. Each word was the beat of my pulse at the time, which quickened as I progressed. Each line I wrote became the rung on a ladder that was needed to climb out of this pit of despair. Each poem became a stepping-stone, moving me forward to what lie ahead. I knew I needed to find a rock to cling to. Like a drowning man, I did find that rock and was able to move forward.

More than 20 poems are strategically placed within the book. None have ever been published. I always felt they were too personal and private to share. Some will include a picture; this is the best visual I can offer you my mindset at the time. For most poems I include an opening note of what prompted the writing and at the end, what was the result of that effort.

In addition, as I was writing I kept an open mind. At times words would flow and I would include them right in the narrative. Some are lines repeated from a poem on previous pages. Many are not. The words, I believe, are inspired by God. I feel they are like a golden thread that ties this book together. I am truly blessed.

Prologue

We are truly blessed by human life. Those we love, those we dream about, those we share our life with. But let us also cherish the animals. They also are a blessed part of this creation.

Here are two quotes from the Bible. (All quotes in this book are from the King James Version of the Bible. Each time I use a quote I will put (KJV) at the end of the quotation):

Job12:7 "But ask now the beasts, and they shall teach thee; and the fowls of the air, and they shall tell thee." (KJV)

Job35:11 "Who teacheth us more than the beasts of the earth, and maketh us wiser than the fowls of heaven?" (KJV)

I will share two books that helped me enormously. Both involve animals. I experienced animal sightings during the death of both Virginia and Rosanna. Each was a different animal. I believe God sends us what we need at the time and this is proof of his constant care. I will share my views on animals and how they helped me in several chapters.

Patricia Spork's book – "Loss Comfort & Healing from Animal Sightings: True Experiences of Animal Blessings" (Booklocker, March 2004)

Steven D. Farmer "Animal Spirit Guides" helped to identify the meaning of the animals sighted. (Hay House Inc. 10/1/2006)

Households today have many varied pets. I think these animals are important. Today we hear about watching the animals that give us indications before an earthquake. I think this is something we should continue to be paying attention to and making an effort to recognize more and more in our lives.

Consider also, the use of service dogs to help those disabled or to calm hospital patients. We continue to find new ways to put God's creatures to good use.

Noah and the Ark. Think of the detailed instructions Noah received. How long, wide and high to make it, what wood to use and what to use to seal it. I saw a TV documentary once that showed a scaled down version was put into a wave tank and they couldn't tip it over. Also, Noah didn't have to go out and round up the animals, they came to him.

God has taken great care of his creation, both human and animal. I think our lives are forever intertwined.

I Kings 17: 2, 4 "And the word of the Lord came unto him saying, and it shall be, that thou shalt drink of the brook; and I have commanded the ravens to feed thee there." KJV)

My first poem was inspired by one of God's creatures. It started me on the road to healing and I have not stopped writing since.

CHAPTER 1

Meeting Virginia

Somehow I knew that when the time came I would meet someone special. I entered the military right after High School because there was a draft on and I didn't want to find myself getting a job or in school and have to leave it for the draft.

While serving in Europe I would frequently think of what an ideal wife would be like. I hoped it would be someone I could love and she would want me in her life as well. I could trust God to make this happen.

(We all make wishes; my wish early on was to
find someone to spend my life with)

Wishes

We all lament the things that could have been,
Or wish we could have glimpsed things unseen;
Or heard unspoken words before things done,
Or felt a sense of love when there was none.

Or tasted victory more times than defeat,
Or swallowed spoken words in battle heat;
Or touched someone unreachable just one time,
Or left no stone unturned when in our prime.

Or climbed into our dreams that certain night,
Or fought the battle fiercer for that right;
Or smelled more sweet successes than despair,
Or took more chances than we should dare.

Wishes are dreams that sometimes come true,
Remember then, we should not make a few;
Wishes unanswered deprive us of hope,
Wishes are endless and that's how we cope.

(Meeting Virginia was the fulfillment of this wish)

After returning from my tour of duty in Europe with the Army, I didn't go out much as I adjusted to civilian life.

I met Virginia Allen in Boston, at a church related youth function in September 1956. She was introduced to me by my sister Catherine, who knew her for several years. For me, it was love at first sight. Her big brown eyes were what I noticed first. I watched her as she interacted with other people in the room, so out-going. Rehearsals were going on for an upcoming stage event for the holidays. Virginia was participating. She was so capable and talented. Being nerdy and withdrawn I would be attracted to her.

She was from tough New England stock. Family members were early workers at the Sandwich Glass Factory, in Sandwich, MA. The family had many educators, some worked at the Perkins School for the Blind.

Virginia sang in the Choir at Trinity Church located in Copley Square in Boston's Back Bay area. The church was founded in 1733. I remember going to hear the choir sing on several occasions, including Christmas and Easter. She had a lovely Mezzo Soprano voice.

The Christian Science Church played an important role in our lives. My mother was healed of Tuberculosis when I was a toddler. Virginia's families were also members. My mother and father both worked there, as well as my sister Cathy. My mother and sister worked at the Publishing House and my father with the Mother Church security offices.

The Original Mother
Church built in 1895

The Extension
built in 1905

Christian Science was founded by Mary Baker Eddy in 1879. This is the world headquarters. There are branches in many countries around the world. This area looks far different now than it did in 1956 when I was living in the area with my parents. The church was surrounded by apartments and stores. The apartment buildings owned by the church and rented to many of their employees.

Virginia shared an apartment nearby with a friend Priscilla. They both also worked for the Publishing House in different offices.

As we dated, we enjoyed walking around the Back Bay area. Boston is such a great city for walking, historical sites around every corner. We dated on a regular basis for several months.

Right away I felt something was happening. She met my parents several times as they all worked at the same place. They thought she was very nice.

Together, we visited her family in Wellesley Hills several weekends a month. She had 3 older sisters all married with children and 2 brothers one older and one younger. She was the youngest daughter. I met them all and loved to watch them all together, they got along so well.

Virginia's father, Roland was an interesting man. He was a World War 1 Veteran and was a lumberjack in Seattle before he met his wife Wilomena in New York State. She was a school teacher and Roland and his brother operated a farm nearby. He also was well known for his woodworking. He made antique Colonial Reproductions, individual pieces and also entire rooms of furniture. He had his shop in the basement.

Every time I visited I would spend time watching him work. Being a klutz I had an appreciation for anyone who had this talent. I asked lots of stupid questions, I'm sure. But he had patience and loved talking about it.

Virginia and I expressed love for each other. I told her I was going to ask her father for her hand in marriage on the next visit. She was happy with this, but we both were a little nervous.

On the next visit, I headed to the cellar as usual. Her father and I talked for a while; he was making dove-tails which they use to hold pieces of wood together rather than using nails or screws. I was standing behind him and said "Sir" He thought I had another stupid question, but turned around. I continued, "I would like to ask you for Virginia's hand in marriage." He dropped his tools and started pumping my hand. *I thought my arm was going to fall off.* He hugged me and said "Yes, now let's go tell her mother." I followed him up the stairs, he yelled "Wilomena come here". She came in from the kitchen, wiping her hands on her apron. He explained. She hugged me. He then asked Virginia to come down; she had gone up to her room.

What happened next brought tears to my eyes. Virginia descended the staircase. How radiant she looked, a beautiful smile on her face. I then looked at her parents. How pleased and happy they looked as they hugged her. I can only imagine any parent cherishing this moment and being in total agreement.

> *Shorty, the nerd and klutz from Somerville, was now ten feet tall! Did his pumping my hand do this? You know like a car jack?*

In January of 1957, I gave her an engagement ring on her birthday. Meeting her wonderful family was so incredible; they were so warm and welcoming.

We were married in June 1957, in the Congregational Church in Wellesley Hills, MA, with friends, family and co-workers in attendance.

> *…Wishes are dreams that sometimes come true,*
> *…..Remember then, we should not make a few;*

We lived in the Back Bay area where we both walked to work. I worked on the IBM Equipment for a small Insurance Company in Kenmore Square. She worked for the Christian Science Publishing House. My parents lived in an apartment, close by and we visited them often.

Pictures

Erwin with Virginia going out somewhere
(wedding pictures were lost in a flooding).

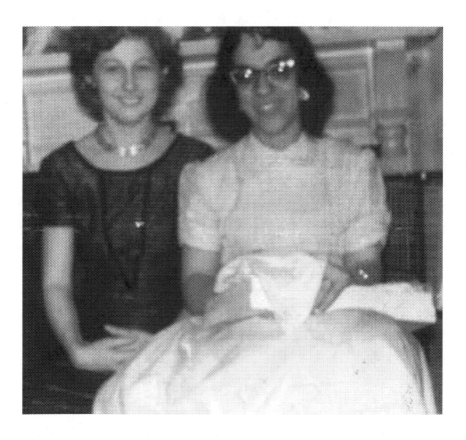

Virginia, with her friend Imogene. They worked
together and Imogene was in her wedding party

(Looking ahead to my future, somehow I knew it would be fulfilling)

Aspirations

I will aspire; I will reach for the sky,
Nothing will hinder my earthly quest;
I will do more than dream, I will try,
You will see me perform my very best.

I will aspire; I will keep an open mind,
Nothing will I withhold from thought;
I will do more than seek, I will find,
I will apply in life all that I'm taught.

I will aspire; I will bare my very soul,
Nothing will stifle my inner passion;
I will do more than achieve my goal,
I will view the world with compassion.

I will aspire; I will have an open heart,
No one will I withhold from my love;
I will do more than care, I will impart,
All negative things I will rise above.

(Looking back I have not been disappointed)

Chapter 1 Summary

Some comments to help you turn some of these negatives into positives.

1. **Commitment**. Along with love, there is also honesty, trust and selflessness. You are investing in each other. We had a common interest in church; this was something we both enjoyed not only in attendance but any activities.

2. **Marriage**. Is not for everyone. Things change over the years, with different trends and norms. I think a lot has to do with the increase in divorces. Many people are hurt, including the children, this effects the decisions they make later. In our families there were no divorces. I felt Virginia and I needed to be committed. Virginia wouldn't have it any other way. Marriage does that. It felt right for us both. That's how we were brought up. It seems right and if I could go back now I would have done the same thing. It's a couple's choice, so there will be no condemnation here, there are so many elements. Love is the central factor that keeps people together.

3. **Prior Relationships**. Be sure they are officially over. You don't want these coming back to interfere with what you have. It takes courage sometimes to end these. Be honest and up front not only with your loved one, but with yourself. Perhaps your loved one can help in this effort. Support each other. That's what love is all about. Turn negatives into positives

4. **Cherish the family you meet**. I became best friends with one of my brother-in-laws. They will be there to support you in need. They are great to spend the holidays with. We learn from each other.

5. **If you are young.** Getting a good education and getting into a good profession is top priority. You are establishing a basis for a long and happy relationship. I was very fortunate working with IBM Accounting Machines, this was the basis for their first computers and I was on the ground floor of a budding industry

6. **If you are older**, most of this has already been established. Support each other in your work, if one wants to change careers

or try for a higher position, be sure to talk this over offering whatever advice or support you can. Sometimes going back to school is in order. This may require sacrifices from both of you.

7. **Appreciation.** Appreciate those who are happy that you made this important decision. My sister Cathy introduced me to Virginia when I went to this church function for the first time. She is three years older than I am. I finally got around to thanking her this year (at age 80). This should have occurred much earlier. Sometimes it's the little things in life we overlook that are important

8. **Cherish your roots.** Looking back I am so thankful for the church members and Sunday School teachers who remained in my life for many years. I recall receiving letters and brownies from some of them during my tour of duty in Europe. In fact, one passed away and his wife continued to communicate with me. If your roots were not pleasant or if there were issues, deal with these early. You don't want to harbor any hate or anger, I feel this will only hinder your progress. If this was the case, talk to someone you trust or read books that may help you move forward.

9. **Treasure Chest**. This is where you place all those wonderful memories, pictures and events in your life. You will look to these all through your life repeatedly. Keep adding to this collection.

CHAPTER 2

Marriage to Virginia

Prior to our marriage we committed to not argue. That all our disagreements would be worked out before we go to bed. We saw so much of this, in families, with friends and neighbors. That this was important and we would strive to make sure this never took place.

Promises

Lord, in marriage we vowed each night,
We won't go to sleep if we had a fight,
We'd get it worked out or wouldn't sleep,
You help those things that mutter and peep.

Get out that hook, stretch out this day,
Put in my mouth the words to say;
I made a promise that I must keep,
The things I said did make her weep.

Hold up that Sun, don't let it set,
We haven't resolved our problem yet,
I made a promise that I must keep,
When you sow you get what you reap.

Hold up that Moon, don't let it rise,
I just got caught in one of those lies;
I made a promise that I must keep,
Problems like these soon make a heap.

Lord, its ok now were doing fine,
That was close, we walk a fine line;
I made a promise that I must keep,
Thanks for helping, now we can sleep.

We lived in an apartment on Peterborough Street. It was close to the area known as "The Fens", a beautiful area of greenery and pleasant areas for walking.

Virginia always wanted a miniature poodle. We shopped around and found Pierre, beautiful silver Miniature Poodle. He is featured in a picture on pages later in this chapter.

Virginia was able to walk to work at the Publishing House and I walked the other direction to Kenmore Square where I worked for a small Life Insurance Company. Every day I walked right by the famous Fenway Park where the Boston Red Sox played.

In late 1957 we found out that Virginia was pregnant. Both families were excited. This would be the first grandchild for my father and mother. Our son Geoffrey was born in the apartment in June 1958. Virginia represented the true Allen family pioneer spirit; as he was born by natural birth.

In Massachusetts, at the time doctors were allowed to make home visits to perform births, as long as they were connected to a hospital, in case of problems. We also had a nursing service for one week for the baby and new mom. The senior nurse stayed 3 days then left the assistant to continue with the new baby and mom. I was in attendance of the birth and will say there is nothing like seeing your own child born. I was able to go to work while the nurses took care of everything.

I have wonderful memories of Geoff growing up. Frequently, Virginia would walk to meet me as I headed home from work. Geoff in a stroller, with Pierre on leash. She often packed a picnic and we would go to the Fens area, sit on the grass while Geoff and Pierre chased each other around. We also would go to the Esplanade on the Charles River. This is where the Boston Pops, led by Arthur Fiedler would play; we sat on the grass and listened to this beautiful music.

We lived in the Boston area for three years. We then looked to move to the suburbs. We found a location south of Boston about 28 miles away. It was a new development in Whitman MA. It was well known for a restaurant called the Toll House. They were known for the Toll House Cookie, so popular today. The new community composed of about 20 new homes. All the families were young many with children. It was exciting to meet new young neighbors and we quickly became friends with many wonderful people.

Shortly after arriving in Whitman we were blessed with the birth of our second son Gregory. We were in the same zone of availability of the doctor used earlier and the same nursing service. Again the senior nurse staying 3 days and then the student stayed the rest of the time tending to the baby and new mom.

We began attending the Christian Science church in nearby Rockland. It was a short drive and we quickly settled into a regular routine exploring the area each week to see what was going on.

About 13 months after the birth of Gregory, we had our third and final son Gary. Again using the same doctor and nursing service. Since Gregory and Gary were so close they played well with each other, both looking up to their big brother Geoff and of course Pierre who welcomed them both.

One thing both Virginia and I loved about New England, was the history and the many traditions. We loved: Christmas Caroling on Beacon Hill or visiting the Boston Common at Christmas time. We lived not far from Plymouth. One Thanksgiving we had dinner right across from where a replica of the Mayflower was docked. We were able to look out the window and see the Mayflower as we dined. The waiters and waitresses were clothed as Pilgrims. This was quite memorable.

During each summer, we would spend time camping all over New England. We visited Lake Dunmore in Vermont often. We had family gatherings in Truro on Cape Cod. We had a tent trailer plus a tent for the boys. We tried to make all the trips educational as much as possible. We even ventured into Canada, camping in their beautiful Provincial Parks. The highlights there, being New Brunswick, Cape Breton, and Prince Edward Island.

When the boys were in school we took historical camping trips to Gettysburg, Valley Forge and to the Smithsonian Institute in Washington DC. The highlights in Washington; being the Lincoln Memorial and the Smithsonian where we saw Lindbergh's plane and some of the early rockets from NASA. Washington has so much history that you can spend weeks there.

Three years after our marriage Virginia lost her father. It was a sad event for me; he was an inspiration and loved by everyone.

> *Our loved ones, precious in our lives,*
> *May have long vanished from our view;*
> *Yet their qualities are still with us,*
> *And continue in memories not a few.*
>
> *Imagine, their light still brightly shines,*
> *We still feel their warmth and tenderness;*
> *Sense the strength of their presence, how*
> *They blessed us with joy and happiness.*

Virginia had a long-time friend Imogene. She was in her wedding party. Once or twice a month I would take her and the boys into Boston, drop off Virginia so she and Imogene could go to dinner, do some shopping and spend some quality time together. Meanwhile, I would take the boys to a penny arcade or to some park where we would throw the ball around. This went on for several years.

After 10 years or so we outgrew our first home and bought another also in Whitman. This was an old farmhouse with a barn. The rest of the property was sold off for development.

Virginia's mom Wilomena found that she needed to go back to work to help provide income. She and my mother worked in the same office for a number of years. They had lunch together every day and became the best of friends. They didn't know each other until Virginia and I met.

Virginia and I were very active in a Christian Science church in Rockland MA which was only a few miles away. At age 28, I was elected First Reader which was quite an honor. I was the youngest First Reader ever for that branch church at the time. My responsibilities were to conduct a service each Sunday and Wednesday evening for a 3 year period. It was wonderful that Virginia supported me during this period. It meant a lot to have someone to share this huge responsibility. My parents were also proud and came to visit the church often. I had to do a lot of studying. I was so fortunate living in the old farmhouse; it had a walk-in pantry where I would go to perform this. I remember the boys being young and knocking on the door to come in. When I look back I'm amazed I was able to accomplish this as well as work full time.

Virginia's mom retired and came to live with us for a while. One day returning from shopping we found she was outdoors with no coat on, it was 17 degrees. We contacted her oldest daughter, Connie and she found a home for her where she would be cared for and watched. In a year or so she passed away. She too was greatly loved.

> ...Hostess at the meals and the breaking of the bread,
>   ... Through the peaks and valleys she was the common thread.

In 1978, we moved to Canoga Park, California. We had visited my parents in the Bay area where they moved after retiring. We loved California, and I relocated to work for Transamerica in Los Angeles. I was in LA for three months looking for a home and getting settled. I was so proud of Virginia for handling the sale of our home and one car and organizing the flight to LA for herself and the three boys. At this point Geoff was in High School and the other two boys in Middle School.

We hated leaving New England and family. Having been brought up there, it is so filled with history and wonderful events. Boston is very cold in the winter and very humid in the summer.

It takes courage to make a major move in our lives; this was certainly the case here. But this was a career move for me. It would lead to many work adventures in Information Technology.

> *...I will aspire; I will reach for the sky,*
> *...Nothing will hinder my earthly quest;*
> *... I will do more than dream, I will try,*
> *...You will see me perform my very best.*

We made another move to Simi Valley CA, we visited there often. We then joined the Thousand Oaks Christian Science church.

Since I had been a First Reader it qualified me to join the California Chaplains Program. After going through a training program I served as Christian Science Chaplain at Camarillo State Hospital for several years before it closed. I also visited young men at the Fire Camps in several counties. The young men were on the way out of the Correction System and would be returning home. They would receive training as fire fighters which could be a huge career because of the numerous fires in the LA area and throughout California. I believe this practice is continued today. I enjoyed meeting with these young men. They were so happy to be nearing the end of this phase of their life and ready to start a new phase. I was pleased they were so hopeful. We were not allowed to follow up with them after they left, but I often wondered how they were doing.

Virginia loved art. She went back to school after raising her family. She received a BA in art, from California State University, Northridge, CA. Her best medium was murals. When the children were growing up she would paint floor-to-ceiling murals in their bedrooms. Ships under full sail; outer-space, including some planets; animals of all sorts. The boys loved these and were always eager to show them to their friends. When we moved to California, the first home we owned had a large blank wall by the entry way. She loved the California Missions and painted a mission scene on this wall. Visitors were impressed.

We loved exploring California and made as many trips as possibly. Virginia had no relatives in California. I had my mother and father as well as my sister Jan with her husband Ted and their children. We visited them often.

On one visit for Thanksgiving we spent the day with Jan, my sister and Ted her husband. My father and mother who lived nearby were at the dinner also. After Thanksgiving dinner I went for a walk with Ted and my father. My mother had recently experienced a mild stroke. As we walked, my father said "I don't think I'm going to be around at the end of the year". Ted and I stopped in our tracks and asked "What do you mean?" He said "Just a feeling I have".

When we gathered to leave to drive home we said our goodbyes. My father gave me the longest and tightest hug I can ever recall. I mentioned it to Virginia on the drive home.

Two weeks before Christmas I received a call from Ted stating that my father had a massive heart attack and was pronounced dead at the hospital. I was stunned; my father had predicted his own demise. I then recalled the hug; long, hard and sweet.

...We look for precious diamonds buried in the ground
... But are often surprised when that's not where they're found

21

After my father's death it seemed impossible for my mother to carry on alone. We volunteered to care for her. She was part of our family for several years. She was able to care for herself and the stroke did not interfere with her eating.

One Saturday I went with a friend to a hockey game. The Boston Bruins were in town to play the LA Kings. When I arrived home, Virginia said "check on your mom". When I went in to see her it was evident she was gone. She died quietly in her sleep, no outcry, no thrashing about. Losing a mother must be the saddest event in anyone's life. It sure was for me.

> *…Mother, what a lovely name and such a gentle soul…*
> *…It takes an angel to fulfill such a role…*
> *…Centered in my life as an everpresent light…*
> *…. Is now a star in heaven shining through the night*

Virginia and I had a good marriage and had no conflicts. We vowed early in our marriage, that if there were any problems we would stay up all night if we had to discuss it. The all-nighters never happened.

Pictures

Erwin's parents Hannah and
Earl dressed for a Masonic Event

Virginia's parents Wilomena
and Roland Allen

Pierre and Geoffrey

Sons Gary, the youngest,
Gregory and Geoffrey the oldest

Chapter 2 Summary

Some comments to help you turn some of these negatives into positives.

1. **Family**. During our marriage, we tried to participate in as much togetherness as possible. We also wanted the boys to be aware of the history involved. In my day most moms stayed at home. My mother never worked while we were growing up, but did later. Today it is very common for both mother and father to be working. If there are no children, this is a good time to stock funds away to be used later. When there are children, child care has to be of importance. Some use close relatives because of the trust factor. Also expenses are a factor. It is important that both partners establish what works best for you both. Today we even have stay at home dads.

2. **Traditions**. We loved them all. I think this is the cement that keeps families together. In New England it was not hard to find a tradition that you could cling to and repeat as often as possible. I think it's a great way to teach children and give them wonderful memories. Learn the traditions where you live. If you have none, seek some way to participate. I suggest on Christmas Eve for example, before you settle down to your own routine. That everyone hop into the car and go out to seek some homeless people. Sing them a Christmas Carol and perhaps give them some homemade cookies. Think of what memories you will bring back into their lives. You are turning negatives into positives and perhaps establishing a wonderful tradition. You have love in your life, share it with others.

3. **Travel.** We liked camping. However, I find that none of our boys do that today. I think they had a good time, but have discovered other things. I liked camping because it was not expensive and we tried to make every trip educational. We had a special place on Cape Cod where we went during the summer. Virginia's family would have six tents most of the time and the cousins all loved playing together. Being around the campfire

at night was very special. Visiting Canada was a real treat. They are wonderful neighbors.

4. **Church**. Not everyone goes to church. I think this is important and I'm glad it was a big part of both of our lives. To have her support while being elected to an important position as First Reader helped me to be able to finish my term with joy. I also had support from my manager where I worked. He was delighted when I told him and was very understanding when I needed time off to perform some church activity. I recommend anyone who is a church goer to be as active as you can. Somehow you will find time needed and certainly the respect of those around you. For those who do not attend church, I would suggest you find some way to attain the peace and happiness that I feel church brings into your life.

5. **Moving.** Everyone finds the need to move when you outgrow your current residence. To relocate across the country as we did is a super move. Not only leaving those behind but meeting new people and new adventures. It takes courage for all involved. I was so proud of Virginia for making this move. She had a lot to do on her end before leaving. I'm sure the boys hated to leave friends, but to this day none have gone back to live there.

6. **Moms and Dads**. Each situation is different on who should step up to care for either one. It is not an easy task. Paramount is the ability to do so and help with their comfort and care. You should have a family meeting or conference call to discuss the pros and cons. I currently live with my son Geoff. I have my own room and bath; have meals with them every day. I get to see the grandkids every day as well. In my estimation this is as good as it gets. I get to go out alone sometimes which I cherish, but love the reception from the grandkids when I arrive back home. This effort can be a problem for some families if there were any prior problems with relationships. It is a subject sometimes discussed and planned ahead. Turn any negatives into positives. They cared for you growing up,

consider caring for them when it becomes time for that to occur.

7. **You're Treasure Chest**. Continue to replenish it with new memories, pictures and life events. This is an important part of life and will be there when you need it.

CHAPTER 3

Losing Virginia

Losing a loved one has to be one of the hardest things to endure. At this point Virginia and I had been married 35 years. I hear of many who never recover. I'm so thankful I had a good religious upbringing; I'm not sure how others manage to move beyond this.

The News Nobody Ever Wants to Hear

We both had always been in good health, although I suffered from asthma. After Virginia began experiencing some discomfort, as usual we turned to a Christian Science Practitioner. This went on for a while with no results. We began to worry and decided to visit a nearby doctor. This was one of the hardest decisions of our life. She went for testing at a hospital nearby.

We visited the doctor's office to get the results; I stayed in the waiting room. After a few minutes the doctor called me in. He said," Virginia, the results of the testing shows that you are in advanced stages of Ovarian Cancer. I estimate that you have about 90 days". We looked at each other in disbelief. He suggested a second opinion.

When we returned to the car, we sat there for a while still stunned. How could this be?

A second opinion was requested, with the same results. Exploratory surgery was recommended to confirm the invasion of the cancer. This was completed and the results confirmed.

The Final Months

Where to begin? Family members needed to be notified, plans made. Her comfort was my priority. I was able to continue to go to work each day, I made arrangements to contact her at specific times so we were connected. We talked about notifying her family. She was reluctant to do this. We also needed to talk to our sons. Suddenly all priorities are changed. How do we put this into words for our boys?

For some reason Virginia was reluctant to talk to her sisters and brothers. I think she didn't want them to worry about her. I couldn't let this happen they needed to know. So I called her brother and sisters to let them know. I told them the terrible news and the best time to contact her. Over the next few weeks, all of them talked to her at least once. Several sisters called her multiple times.

I talked to my sons and told them to come by to see her. It was not easy to break the news to them. Gregory was living with us at the time going to a local community college. They all agreed they would do this.

At this point Gary the youngest, was involved with helping his wife, Grace, she was battling Colon Cancer. We had gone to Phoenix to visit her a month or so before.

I called the oldest, Geoffrey, he promised to come by. All the boys were in disbelief.

It was important to keep her occupied and keep her mind off the problem. We would make day trips to our favorite places. She was able to go upstairs to our bedroom. I rented a wheelchair so we could go out and not tire her out with the trips. We went to the mall several times. It helped her to get out and see people.

There were no hospice services available at the time, this developed later. The doctor was impressed that I was willing to take care of her. He told me that I would be surprised how many people would just walk away.

I couldn't do this to her. I think this helped in his finding nurses, who would make home visits that I could use.

The final weeks

I was in panic mode. I was able to work, enveloping my thoughts with whatever work was at hand. During this time, she talked to me about not staying single that I should remarry. I didn't want to talk about it – she was my priority. This would come up several times during the following weeks. I'm not sure why this was a priority for her; perhaps to make sure I would be taken care of.

The pets were confused, someone different feeding them at odd times. There were late evening trips for pickles and Chinese Food, just like when she was pregnant. Whatever she wanted, I didn't hold anything back. After a while the smell of food began to nauseate her. I was careful not to cook anything that would cause an aroma, because eating became a problem

Several friends came to visit. Geoffrey and Gary came and spent some time with her. I never asked what they discussed. I can only imagine a final visit with my own mother. Gregory, who lived at home with us, had yet to go see her. During this time it was uncomfortable for her to negotiate the stairs. So she was isolated to the upper floor. I would make sure she had everything she needed before leaving for work and called her several times. My sister Jan came to stay with me for a couple of weeks. She was a big help, when she had to leave to tend to her own family, I was able to get a Visiting Nurse to drop by daily and be on call. She was given a morphine pack to wear and could inject herself as needed for the pain. I think this helped.

She was restricted to the upstairs bedroom. There was no way she would be able to use the stairs. Our bedroom was comfortable but had only a single upper window that looked out on some trees close to the house. This was the only link to the outside world. I often wondered what she would think about. Occasionally I would see a smile on her face.

The Window

She sat from dawn to dusk those many hours,
The window her link to those leafy bowers;
And watched as birds flew from limb to limb,
Till cherished daylight hours began to dim;
She yearned to join the human race again,
In world's that lay beyond that window pane.

Billowed clouds would move across the sky,
Changing shape as on their courses ply;
Storms would bring to all their heavy load
Till the streams and rivers over-flowed;
Answered prayers of farmers for their grain,
Drops would trickle down that window pane.

The night flock the star-shepherd tends,
Would send greetings from long lost friends;
At times the chair would start to rock,
Till it timed with the ticking of the clock;
For years the Moon has traveled in its reign,
Shining its light through that window pane.

Memories from long ago would come to mind,
And bring a smile, rich as molten gold refined;
Pleasant thoughts would brighten up the room,
Till every corner freed itself of heavy gloom;
And joy lost long ago came from whence it lain,
And rested on this side of the window pane.

The final days

I took time off from work to be with her. We spent each evening together, talking and watching television. I couldn't begin to think about life without her. It was like a bad dream and kept hoping I would wake up. She was worsening each day. At this point we were into 75 days after the doctor's report.

I spent time downstairs each day trying to be quiet so she could sleep. I made frequent trips upstairs to check on her. The phone was not ringing; I kept in touch with family members on a regular basis.

Gregory still had not gone in to see her. I caught up with him when he arrived home one evening and told him he needed to go see her, it was important and something he would regret later if not done. He went to see her that night and spent some time. She passed away that night. I think his visit was what she was waiting for. I had promised her I would keep in touch with all three boys.

   ….Get out that hook, stretch out this day…
   ….Put in my mouth the words to say…

The final hours

We lay in bed holding hands. I was watching TV. At some point I fell asleep. When I awoke I noticed that she was no longer gripping my hand. I checked on her and found she was not breathing. I kissed her on the forehead and told her that I loved her. I then covered her with the sheet and hugged her one final time.

She died on a Sunday in September in the bed her father had made for her and where she had birthed her three sons. I went down stairs to call the Coroner's Office, a prearranged number I was given to report to them.

I then sat in the dark living room, staring off into space until daylight. My darling girl was gone. I was alone with God. Her lovely soprano voice had been silenced.

...remember the Sabbath Day...oh God...I will...

My sister Jan was with me after the Coroner's Office had picked up Virginia. We were standing in the living room looking out the window. We saw a huge turtle walking down the middle of the road. How out of place it looked, where did it come from? How strange it looked. The street was not a main thoroughfare but busy. This will stay in my memory.

Final arrangements and her final request

Virginia did not want a funeral service. She wanted friends and family to go out to dinner and talk about the good times. We did this, we talked and laughed and cried. She also requested to be cremated and her ashes scattered at sea. I was contacted by the Funeral Director when her ashes were ready so we could arrange to go have her scattered. I told him I couldn't go; it was too painful for me. He said he understood and would take care of it. I felt terrible but thankful that she spared me having to attend a service.

I heard from some who attended the dinner later, they all indicated that it was not enough closure for them. I thanked them, but was grateful that I did not have to go through that ordeal.

*(After Virginia's passing, I would drive to the
seashore, park my car and think of her)*

The Next Wave

To all who lost a loved one far at sea,
Or ashes gently scattered set them free;
We gaze upon the waters and hope to find
Something there that will forever bind;
For us the waves of time are ever beating,
The next wave for us a tender greeting.

Birds that fly high above the sea will soar
To view them there - then return to shore;
If we visit there - this is a priceless bond,
Upon us all this fresh new day has dawned;
For us, the joys of life were fleeting,
The next wave for us a precious greeting.

The fish that swim in deepest ocean depth,
Meet with them - return where shoals are kept;
If we visit there, we share this bonding too,
We have a vigil, an appointed rendezvous;
For us, each wave will be a happy meeting,
The next wave for us a joyful greeting.

The shells and seaweed from the ocean floor,
Wrap around them before washing ashore;
If we visit there and gently touch these few,
We're satisfied and sense their presence too;
For us each wave our love repeating,
The next wave for us a gentle greeting.

(The visits there diminished as I began to feel comfortable about her)

My darling girl was gone forever. My life as I knew
it was over. How can I go on without her?

…When does the solace come to take away my pain?
….Who administers the balm to make me whole again?
….Who fills this emptiness I'm feeling in my heart?
….Where is the Comforter, how soon will it start?

The aftermath

I was totally lost. I took long walks, sitting occasionally and staring off
into space. I was looking for some way to help myself. I knew there was
a rock within that I could cling to, but how to find it was my problem.
I don't know how I was able to go to work every day. Friends and
coworkers were very understanding.

There were thoughts of suicide that lasted a couple of days. I remember
walking into the garage several times to look at the beams, to see if any
would hold my weight. At the time, my son Gregory was living with
us. The thought disappeared, when I realized I couldn't have him come
home to find this. He would be traumatized for life.

The long walks helped to center my thought. When I returned home
each time I would write down my thought. These began taking on a
poetic form.

My enemy is an empty mind,
Images lurk in hidden places;
Want to be in the limelight,
I need to see happier faces.

I need to flood my mind
With wonderful recollections;
These need to be center stage
I will make these selections.

(This was the first poem written after Virginia's death. One day while walking I sat on a bench for a while, staring off into space. Feeling depressed and not knowing where to begin making sense of Virginia's passing, I looked down, and saw a Caterpillar walking beneath. I wondered if it knew that he would someday be a Butterfly. This was the first step in uplifting my thought and prompted this poem, written in the few days that followed)

Transformation

Wooly Caterpillar, creeping on the ground,
Do you know now, where you are bound?
Is there a secret hidden in your mind,
Someday soon leaving all this behind?
Soon you'll shed the body you know,
And gossamer wings of beauty will grow;
Then you will flutter above the earth,
Distant far from your mortal birth;
And through this change be set free,
Finally, what God wants you to be.

Earth-bound man, pacing to and fro,
Do you know now, where you will go?
Is there a secret hidden in your mind,
Someday soon leaving all this behind?
Then in the twinkling of an eye,
Before you different paths will lie
Soon you will leave the body that you bare,
And take on a shape divinely fair;
Through this transformation things unfold,
Finally, completely what God has mold.

(This transformation, resulting in a beautiful butterfly, which now was able to fly and flutter around as if to say – "Look at me, I'm more beautiful now and free". This comforted me to think that Virginia had gone through a transformation as well and could now say the same)

(One night, several days after Virginia's passing, I had a dream. I saw her walking on the shore of a shiny river. This prompted the following poem)

There is a River

There is a river shining bright,
I saw it in a dream one night;
I saw you standing on the shore,
You looked beautiful as before;
I felt no sense of great concern
Someday soon I will return,
We'll walk again in the moonlight;
By that river I dreamed one night,

Wait for me on that distant shore,
We'll walk again just as before;
I will be there by your side,
As I was when you were my bride;
I need not worry anymore,
I saw you waiting on the shore,
By that river I dreamed one night,
By that river shining bright.

(This was an important event. I saw her walking, not worried or suffering. This comforted me greatly. It was an indication that she was safe and alright)

(This was the beginning of facing reality and contemplating facing the future. What will happen next? How do I move ahead?)

Winters Crop

Virginia died. Life now, seems cold
and desolate, the winter of my life is here;
Dreams shattered of together growing old,
Too soon has come the time I greatly fear.

How can I go on without her now?
How empty is this canyon in my heart;
"Till death do us part" seems a distant vow,
Somehow we thought we'd never be apart.

But after winter, comes the spring and warm
Sunshine, and from the earth comes life
With beauty and smells and buds that form
Patterns on the landscape with an artists' knife.

I can look to these and follow through;
The dreams we had can be reborn;
This gives me hope, strength and things to do,
And from this comes purpose. Virginia lives.

(It was time for me to keep busy and not dwell on past experience)

Chapter 3 Summary
Some comments to help you turn some of these negatives into positives.

1. **Caring for a loved one.** There is no place like home. Hospice care as it is known today was not available at this time. I was fortunate to have a sister who could come to help and had a Visiting Nurse available

2. **Suicide**. For me this lasted only two days. If you have thoughts of suicide please discuss this with someone close to you. Here is the National Suicide Prevention Hot Line 1-800-273-8255. Don't let your current feelings deprive you of the blessings that may be in store for you in the months or years ahead. You will see in the chapters ahead that I would have been greatly deprived of much joy and happiness. Think of those left behind. Especially if they will be the one to find you should you follow through with this event. Turn this negative into a positive. You can trust God to help you.

3. **Writing Poetry**. I was inspired to write poetry. I didn't start writing until Virginia died. Find some way to express your feelings. Even if it is notes or comments or some form of journal. Be inspired; make your loved one proud. What is your source of inspiration?
   The Turtle. **Note**: *At this point in time Pat Spork's Book on "Animal Sightings" and Steven Farmer's book "Animal Spirit Guides" had not been published. Later, my sister Jan sent me The information on the Turtle, from Steve Farmer's book:*
   "If the Turtle shows up:
   - *Take time to nurture yourself and simply observe and feel your emotions*
   - *This a very creative, fertile time and you need to shield yourself from interferences that threatens to distract you*
   - *Spend a few hours or longer in solitude, away from other people and the usual noise that surrounds you*

As it turned out, this is exactly what I did. How did I know this? By luck? Was it instinctive? I believe the latter and it worked.

4. **Final Requests.** Carry out your loved ones last wishes. This is important for both of you. Even if it may not be the best way for other family members. At times I felt cowardly not being up to scatter her ashes. But I think it's understandable.

5. **Final Arrangements.** Cherish those who attend any services. They are there for you because they love you. Don't obsess over those not present. They feel worse about not attending than you do. There are so many reasons and factors involved. My son Gary had his hands full with his wife Grace being hospitalized. My son Geoffrey felt terrible about not being able to come. But you will learn in upcoming chapters why and what he has been able to accomplish since then. Turn any negatives into positives

6. **Handling grief.** Everyone handles this differently. I'm not sure if counseling was available at the time. I knew I had a rock within that I needed to find. Thank God I was able to do this. But not everyone is so fortunate

7. **Faith tested.** It was a real disappointment not to have the healing we desired. I'm sure any religious person would say the same. At this point in my writing, I am no longer a "practicing" Christian Scientist. However, that doesn't take anything away from what Mary Baker Eddy founded. I still go to her writings for inspiration and insight. Currently I'm reading the Bible cover to cover for the second time. There are many instances where faith has been tested. Even Jesus' disciples failed to heal at times

8. **Treasure Chest.** Keep it filled. At times like this, reach in for a memory or two to keep you uplifted. Lean on other family members for support. Somehow I knew I would be comforted. It's one of the promises from the Beatitudes.

Chapter 4

Meeting Rosanna

Finding Love Again at 57

It was almost inconceivable to me that I would be able to find someone else at my age. All of the dating norms had changed. Even marriage was not very popular. But as before, I knew I could trust God to somehow lead me to where I needed to be.

You

You came into my life one day and I've never been the same,
You gave me hope once again and set my heart aflame;
You lifted spirits bending low you made me smile once more,
You gave me tender constant care you made my senses soar.

You came into my mind one day and I've never been the same,
You gave me balance once again like pictures in a frame;
You added color to my sight which saw only black and white,
You lit a candle in the dark and took away the night.

You came into my heart one day and I've never been the same,
You rekindled love again and fanned its dying flame;
You welcomed me into your life like fingers in a glove,
You mended my broken heart and strengthened it with love.

You came into my soul one day and I've never been the same,
You gave me joy when there was none you made my anguish tame;
You filled my emptiness with happiness once more,
You took away the pain one day and filled my treasure store.

Drifting

After climbing out of my pit of despair, I began to look for things to do. I knew I needed to keep busy.
I had a lot of time on my hands.

One thing I learned after talking to people who had lost a spouse, is that Virginia wanting to discuss my future and finding someone, was now showing some importance. I met many who never had this discussion and when the time came for them to re-marry they felt guilty about it. Sometimes it was because the subject never came up or it was a sudden death of a loved one, in which they never got a chance to discuss it.

I appreciated many friends and relatives fixing me up with people they knew so I could go out dating again. This was before the Social Websites were available and became popular. I'm not sure I would have used them anyway.

Conversation starters were always a problem. I usually asked how they happen to know the individual who connected us. "So, how long have you known my Uncle Harry?" or "So, Jack from work, how did you know him?"

I usually met for about an hour with all of them. Sometimes it was an interesting conversation other times it went painfully long. There was never enough interest to call any of them back. One I remember the only thing we found in common was that we were using forks to eat.

Although I met many nice people it was getting tiring, I felt like I was drifting and I decided to give it up. I knew that if it was right that I meet someone, it would happen, letting nature take its course.

Little did I know, it would happen and it would happen quickly and completely. I was feeling confident again. I had found the rock within to cling to and under that rock a poetic voice. I can now calm my fears, share my innermost thoughts or yell from the mountain tops.

Meeting Rosanna

After several months I saw an ad in a local paper, the Library was going to be having classes for those interested in tutoring newcomers to the U.S. in English. This interested me, so I signed up. It was four consecutive Saturdays after which they would help to get you assigned to work with someone. I worked full time, but had lots of spare time. After the training I was given a choice of one night a week at the Library or two nights a week working with inner-city kids serving time at the Ventura School. This was the only Co-ed California Youth Authority in California. I opted for this. They were all serving time for crimes committed as a juvenile. As a Chaplain I recalled meeting with young men on the way out of the system and this interested me. They could not come out for tutoring if they had any demerits that week and had to be doing well in school. I felt they were motivated enough and wouldn't be wasting my time. There were about 20 Tutors. The boys and girls were tutored separately. We all met in a common area before getting escorted in and also had to be escorted out. Some nights we had to pass on tutoring because the school was on lock-down and sometime we had to wait to get escorted out because of some incident that occurred while we were there.

There is something about being in a confined environment. To hear the doors "clang" behind you as you make your way to the tutoring area, is something not soon forgotten. The boys I had were interested in moving on. They lost time in school and seeing family. It must be almost impossible for them to see that this is only temporary and they must change when they get out. The home life is always on their mind. I remember one boy telling me he had a baby at home that was approaching its first birthday. He had a card to send but didn't know what to write. I told him to think that this child was sitting right here with him. "What would you say?" He thought for a moment and I left him for a few minutes to look out the window as he wrote. When I returned he was stuffing the card into an envelope, the tears I saw indicated to me that he found the words. I often thought of those I met with and hoped they found the peace within to be able to move on and lead a normal life.

After the tutoring sessions were over, both the students and the tutors had a chance to mingle for a few minutes before they were escorted out. It gave us a chance to meet each other's students and to get to know them a little better. It gave me a chance to observe the other tutors. I was glad we had this time, I'm sure the students loved it as well to be out of their normal activity for a time.

Rosanna was one of the Tutors. The first time I saw her, I couldn't take my eyes off her. Opposites attract, so being nerdy and withdrawn, I'd be attracted to someone with a great personality. Boy, did she have that and a great smile. (She told me later that my staring at her scared the hell out of her) One night as we were on the way out – I asked her if she would like to get a cup of coffee. To my astonishment she agreed. During coffee we both mentioned that we would be traveling the following week to northern California for Thanksgiving to spend with family. We found out later, we were headed in the same direction, to cities that were only 26 miles apart. We could have driven together.

The holidays for me, will be a problem from here on. Virginia and I spent them with family here in California and they were always memorable occasions.

After returning, I met with Rosanna again for coffee. This was the beginning of a short dating period. We began to spend more time together.

(Rosanna's home was in a gated community. There was a garden
exit gate that allowed me to get to my car in the visitor parking)

Life's Mystery's

Sometimes it's hard to understand when life plays out without a rule,
It's hard to understand the rule that works alike on king and fool;
Life seems like an elevator with all its ups and downs,
On and on without a clue who's to say what comes around?

Does Lightning strike the same place twice, is life just a roll of dice?
Can broke hearts be repaired or separate lives be shared so nice;
Who's to say what the future holds or what might be our fate;
Right now there's nothing sweeter than those kisses by the gate.

(While dating, going to my car to leave, made my day)

At the time, I lived in Simi Valley CA and Rosanna lived in Camarillo CA. Our first real date was on New Year's Eve. We went to a movie and saw "A Few Good Men", then went back to her home and had dinner (this was when I realized – wow, what a great cook) we talked and danced all night long. Our conversations covered everything from individual values, work experience, family life and marriage. She admitted to being married several times, I was impressed that she was so open and honest. The next thing we knew it was getting light out.

She asked if I would like some breakfast. I said "Sure". I stayed in the kitchen as she prepared the food. I was impressed how she moved so freely and was so professional at her preparation. It showed that she had been doing this a long time. We had breakfast and watched the Rose Parade. I was not into the dating norms, after having been married so long, so I didn't make any moves. As it turned out it was the best thing I did. She had been physically and verbally abused in a previous marriage and any moves on my part would have freaked her out.

The klutz factor presented itself early in our relationship. I had a headlight out on my car. My usual practice was to drop by an auto store, pick up the replacement and then go to my local garage to have it installed. One evening, I picked up Rosanna to go out to some event. When she entered the car she kicked the headlight that I had picked up and placed on the floor on the passenger side. She said "What's this?" I explained. She said "Hold on" She got out, popped the hood, went to her garage, got a tool box and in 10 minutes had it replaced. I was stunned. Wow, not only does she cook, she can fix stuff!!

During the days that followed I couldn't get her out of my mind. I even called her a few times trying not to seem overeager. Immediately after each time we went out for dinner or coffee, I called my sister Jan to tell her about Rosanna and any new updates. I felt something was happening. I didn't know it at the time, but Rosanna was doing the same, calling her sister in Connecticut to tell her about me.

There was one piece of unfinished business. I was still wearing Virginia's wedding ring. I felt I needed to be committed at this point in my relationship with Rosanna. It had been on my finger 35 years; I couldn't get it over my knuckle. I went to a local jeweler to have it cut off. The "click" I heard will reverberate forever in my memory. When I returned to my car, I sat there awhile and sobbed. The final act - the official ending to our wonderful marriage was overwhelming.

(My thoughts on when it is love)

When Is It Love?

The smile is the outer expression of the heart,
It is an attraction when together or apart;
Its love when all you want to do is smile,
When together or when alone for a while.

The eye is the lens to the inner soul,
From initial eye contact it becomes whole;
Its love when you look into each other's eyes,
And see into the very depth of where love lies.

The nostril is the entry to the hallways of the mind,
Your scent lingers long after we have dined;
Its love when after you've gone I smell your hair,
And its essence is something beyond compare.

The touch is the first indicator of tenderness,
The goosebumps and tingling felt long after;
Its love when you miss this simple act,
And want more because it's what you lack.

The ear is the portal to the private heart,
To hear the laughter or hear your name;
Its love when you hear the words "I love you",
And can't wait to say the same words so true.

Chapter 4 Summary
Some comments to help you turn some of these negatives into positives.

1. **Dating**. Always a question as to how soon. It's going to depend, I think, on the individual. I felt I needed to get out of the house. Also, I had been married 35 years, things change. In my case it was at least two months and the initial dates were blind dates, people recommended to me by my co-workers, relatives or friends.

   Here are some things to consider:
   - **Safety**. Meet in a safe place where you can arrive and leave anytime. I like Starbucks, but they get crowded and noisy. Local malls are good; they have food courts or restaurants where you can order a soft drink and dessert. You want a quiet place where you can stay awhile and talk
   - **Social Websites**. I think this will depend on how tech-savvy you are. The technology is ever changing, so it's hard to keep up with the changes. This may lend itself well for a younger person who is into this more than an older person. One of the factors here is trust. The person represented online may or may not be the person your meeting.
   - **Volunteering**. This is the best in my opinion. One of the things you're looking for is finding something you have in common. If you meet while volunteering you already have that. You can then observe the individual and talk with them. Remember I scared the crap out of Rosanna by staring at her. So you want to go easy, don't be overly anxious. Rosanna and I tutored twice a week, so we saw each other often. I waited several weeks before asking her out for coffee. If the person is unavailable, I think and hope they would say no. You hear so much about stalking these days, so tread lightly.

2. **Handling holidays**. If your loss was close to a holiday, this is always a problem. With Rosanna, she celebrated all the holidays,

with her dining opportunities, so I was in trouble on that. Here's what I can say. My father died close to Christmas, after seeing him at Thanksgiving, I never saw him again. He and my mother went through hard times, but they stayed together. I remember once having no presents under the tree at Christmas and eating catsup sandwiches because that's all we had. Every Christmas was a downer after he died. So, I turned a negative into a positive.

In my father's name at Christmas, or many times during the year, I will do something good for a stranger. It might be giving money, pocket change or a bottle of water to a homeless person. I have ordered flowers or fruit baskets for a neighbor and had it delivered anonymously. Would that make my father proud? You bet!

I had turned a negative into positive.

Virginia's family (Allen's) Every Thanksgiving had a guest at the table. One year it might be a relative who lives alone, a friend they haven't heard from in a while or a neighbor who has no relatives nearby. We continued this practice during our marriage.

VOLUNTEER. VOLUNTEER. Turn a negative into a positive. By blessing others it will get your mind off your own problems.

There is **ALWAYS** someone worse off than you.

CHAPTER 5

Marriage to Rosanna

Getting remarried was special for me. At this point in time in my life, there was always some sense of insecurity. Will it work? Are we truly committed? I had to trust God. It worked for me so far in my life. Why would it not work now?

In my thought it was like morning. Everything is new, everything is refreshed.

Morning

Nothing more refreshing than the morning new,
As we all awake to begin a brand new day;
The past washed in the freshness of the dew
And coldness by the suns warming ray.

Here we have a chance to begin things anew,
The slate is clean and ready for our hand;
The time is opportune to correct or undo,
Is now the time to make that valiant stand?

Here is that day we thought would never come,
Here is that chance we always wanted to seize;
No time now to shake in fear or limbs to numb
Perhaps it should humbly begin on our knees.

Yesterday's problems should be left behind,
No need to take our trash into tomorrow;
We can even love those who've been unkind,
Or throw off that heavy cloak of sorrow.

Nothing more refreshing than the morning new,
As we all awake to begin a brand new day;
For saints, or convicts and even for you,
Nothing can stop it or stand in the way.

When we dated it was seldom going out to eat, she was a great cook and probably found it hard to select a good restaurant, so we ate at her home. This was good because we could discuss work as well as other events in our lives. She lived in a gated community and had over 200 clients as a Financial Planner for American Express. I met some of them at her home when they came to discuss business, but sometimes they invited her out to eat and she brought me along (I think to get their approval later).

We did take day trips to Santa Barbara, Port Hueneme and Oxnard, visiting some of her favorite sites. I had spent time with Virginia in Santa Barbara, so I loved the city as well.

We were getting serious. At this point I've known her only four months. I told her that I would like to marry her. She said, "Even after what you know about me and my previous marriages?" I said, "Yes, I'm not marrying them, I'm marrying you - the you I know". She accepted this, but suggested that we both need to pass the sister test. My sister, Jan and her husband Ted lived in the Southern California area. We had dinner with them. My sister thought she was just great.

It was a little harder with Rosanna's sister, who lived in Connecticut. We talked on the phone several times. She heard that I wrote poetry and we exchanged "silly" poems over email. By the time I did meet her later we were old friends.

By this time, I met Rosanna's son Jay, who lived nearby in another city. We set a date for the wedding and went shopping for rings.

We continued to date and were married in
Thousand Oaks CA on March 13, 1993.

Our Wedding Vows

(Erwin) This ring I place upon your hand,
        Is more than just a golden band;
        It represents my love for you,
        To cherish all the things you do;
        To shield you from impending harm,
        To keep your life serene and calm;
        This ring upon this day we wed,
        Will remind me of these words I said.

Rosanna) This ring I place upon your hand,
        Is more than just a golden band;
        It represents my love for you,
        Patience in all the things you do;
        To reach inside and draw you out,
        When you are quiet with worry or doubt;
        This ring upon this day we wed,
        Will remind me of these words I said.

Reception

Our Marriage

My marriage to Rosanna occurred six months after Virginia's passing. To go from that pit of despair to the mountains top was beyond anything I could imagine. I have a new life and new wife. I was either very lucky or someone is watching over me. I believe the latter.

Here are the strengths that I brought to the marriage

A good sense of humor

I believe I got this from my mother. She had so many ways to make us laugh. I also like to draw cartoons. Rosanna had a good sense of humor as well. Laughter is good for you. There are many books written on this subject. I remember some occasions we were laughing so hard, we had to catch our breaths or were down on all fours.

Here is a couple of books:

Readers Digest "Laughter the Best Medicine"
Milan Kundera "The Book of Laughter and Forgetting"

Stability

Marriage to Virginia for 35 years. Virginia and I vowed early in our marriage to never fight. If there was an issue we would stay up all night to talk it out. The all-nighters never occurred. I wrote the lyrics to a duet I hope to get published one day. "Help Me Find the Words"

Work ethic

After working as an employee for several companies and getting laid off because they moved out of state or went bankrupt, I decided to do consulting work by joining an IT Consulting Firm. I loved this because I was treated as a professional and did my best work.

Shortly after this I became an Independent Contractor and found work around California. I stayed connected with those I worked with and we worked together several times on projects around the state. The work was steady and paid well.

Here is Rosanna's background – she brought so much more to the marriage than I did

Rosanna was born on July 2, 1935, on a farm in Townville, Pennsylvania not far from Pittsburg.

She attended local schools and was a High School Cheerleader.

She had an early interest in music and earned a BA in Music from Westminster College in Pennsylvania.

After moving to California and raising a family, she earned a BA in Geography at Cal State University – Northridge California, and she taught there for a while. Earth Sciences always interested her and concern for the environment. She was one of the first to have an Electric Car, the EV1 from General Motors in 1999. For the years that followed she only owned Hybrid Vehicles.

After earning a degree in Urban Studies at Cal State University – Northridge California, she worked as a City Planner in Ventura County.

She was active and had varied interests - at one point, flew a single-engine plane all over southern California. She also had a 28-foot sailboat sailing around the Channel Islands and Catalina.

Always fascinated in investing - she became a CFP (Certified Financial Planner) and was one of the first woman in her office, to work in that capacity for American Express. She worked as a CFP for 17 years.

Life with Rosanna

At that time she was already involved with women's equality, rights and social justice. She was a 30-year member of AAUW (American Association of University Women), actively serving as an officer while in Sacramento, Riverside and in Palm Springs.

She had a high IQ, qualifying her to join Mensa (High IQ Society). I could never confirm her score. She was an avid reader with membership in three Book Clubs – reading 2-3 books a week was not unusual.

Cooking was Rosanna's passion. She was a Gourmet cook with over 400 recipes. The largest group was Soups & Stews. She loved making soups from scratch. Like most good cooks - she enjoyed the work involved, was not afraid to experiment, didn't need to measure ingredients, had distinctive taste buds and left the kitchen a mess. She loved to garden and planted some of the vegetables and herbs used in her food preparation.

I gave up my apartment and moved into her home in Camarillo CA. The food was incredible, I mean every meal. When I shopped for food for my apartment it was frozen or canned. This was more than I could dream.

Rosanna loved to entertain. We had guests for dinner 2-3 times a month. Some were my co-workers who wanted to meet her. But it included friends, neighbors and those from AAUW or from our church.

Fine dining was all new to me. Rosanna was great at selecting wines for each meal. I was introduced to this early in our marriage and acquired a taste for the wines especially from here in California. We had a wine cooler in the home as she would buy several bottles at a time. This was the first time in my life I was drinking any alcoholic beverages. Rosanna didn't participate because of her medications. But she would carefully watch me. After about a glass of wine I would get a buzz on. I would look across the room and see Rosanna running her hand back and forth across her throat indicating I had had enough. I would wave in acknowledgement. I asked her once what the indicators were. She said, "Your loud laughter or becoming real animated".

Driving while having a buzz on, was never a problem. Rosanna drove everywhere we went. If she was a passenger she would get car-sick, but while driving she was okay. She told me once, "I've been driving since I was 12; I learned to drive a tractor on my family farm." I would comment occasionally when she got into traffic, "Remember, honey you're no longer on the farm".

One day while starting off to work she said, "You're wearing that with that?" I looked down at my clothes with my nerdy, geeky eyes and said, "Wearing what with what?" She said never mind, we are going shopping this weekend.

This was the beginning of a vast improvement in my wardrobe. On that weekend we did go shopping and started a new set of coordinated clothes.

We kept our clothes in separate places in the house. She had a lot of clothes and I was beginning to collect a lot myself. At least twice monthly, when leaving to go out, we would invariably end up wearing the same colors. We both hated that, not wanting to look like twins. So she would then say, "One of us has to change". I never protested, I knew I was going to change. But no problem, I had these Rosanna-approved coordinates in my closet I just had to put on another color.

At work I was getting complements on my clothes. Damn, she was making me look good!!

(We loved to cuddle and did so often)

In Your Arms

There is no place I'd rather be,
Then here within your loving arms;
There is no safer place for me,
From terrible foe or earthly harms.

There is no spell on earth to see,
Than here beneath your lovely charms;
There is no salve that healeth me
Your touch becomes a soothing balm.

There is no place that I could flee
Like tropic isle with waving palms;
No words like yours comforts me
Not angel voice, nor David's Psalms.

(This will turn out to be important – it probably saved my life)

A serious health issue

As mentioned in a previous poem regarding cuddling. We were watching TV one night; Rosanna had her head on my chest. She said "your heart sounds weird." I said "what do you mean?" She said "I'm not sure just doesn't sound right. I think you should make an appointment to have it checked."

My heart was checked by a Cardiologist connected to the Los Robles Medical Center in Thousand Oaks. He ordered a Coronary Angiogram, at the hospital, which injects dye into the veins so the blood flow to my heart can be monitored.

As I lay in the bed, Rosanna and the doctor viewed my heart on the monitor. Rosanna said "Wow", the doctor said "Oh my. He then came to the bed and said "you need to go home and get your toothbrush and report back here at 6:00 PM, you're going into surgery in the morning."

Rosanna told me on the way home that a large portion of my heart was all black showing no flow at all. At this point I was not having any health issues.

After I checked into the hospital to prepare for the surgery, the surgeon came to visit me and assured me that everything would be alright, he had performed over 2,000 of these. In the morning I was taken to surgery. Quadruple Heart Bypass surgery was performed. In addition a birth defect with the Mitral Valve was repaired. A vein was taken from my left leg to be used to replace the clogged veins to my heart.

I don't know how long I was in surgery, it had to be hours. The only thing I remember was being wheeled down the hallway to a room. I could see the lights overhead as we moved. I was also shivering uncontrollably. I didn't know that they pack you in ice or something similar to lower your heart rate. The next thing I knew I saw Rosanna leaning over to look at me. I said "Why the hell am I so cold?" she laughed, I'm sure that was a relief for her, that I had successfully made it through the surgery.

I appreciated those who came to the hospital to visit me. These included one of Rosanna's ex's (Jays father) I was glad to meet him. I was a patient there for about a week before getting released to go home.

What followed was a long rehabilitation period in physical therapy at the Los Robles Medical Center. The Cardiologist informed me on our first visit after the surgery that they noticed scarring on the heart that indicated that I had previous heart attacks. I remember while in the Boston area that I had several severe Asthma attacks, it could have occurred then. I also told him that I had a high pain threshold that allowed me to have dental work performed without Novocain. On the one hand good not to feel pain, but not when you need to feel it.

I was out of work for over three months. I hate to think what would have happened if we had not been cuddling. My father died of a massive heart attack; I was probably headed to the same end.

The TLC I received at home from Rosanna was incredible. We had been married only 5 months when this occurred. I remembered seeing later, one of her Soup Recipes titled, "Chicken Noodle Soup for Sick Erwin".

From here on I would need to watch my diet. Who better to be involved with that than Rosanna? We added fish to our diet and would have it several times a month, and in addition had all veggie plates on occasion.

One of the first trips we made was to visit her sister in Connecticut. We flew to Boston and rented a car to go to her sister's house. When we met we had already communicated on phone and emails but there is nothing like a face-to-face meeting. She was enjoyable. Her sister Marie was recovering from a nasty accident some months earlier. She was raking leaves in her backyard into a pile and burning them. During the process she tripped and fell into the burning leaves. She was badly burned. Rosanna had flown back to be with her and several of her relatives had been staying with her during her recovery. At this point in time she was recovering and was up and about. I loved to watch Marie and Rosanna interact, like any two loving sisters.

While there we visited my sister Cathy and her husband Linwood in Massachusetts. I had not seen her for several years. She was delighted to meet Rosanna and we spent most of the day with her.

Rosanna had been to every state in the country except Maine. So before flying back home we drove to Maine for a Lobster dinner. I had been away from the New England area at this point 15 years. It was nice getting back there for a visit.

Rosanna retired from American Express. We lived in various locations wherever I was finding work. In 1998 we moved to the Sacramento area, I was working on Y2K, serving as Test Coordinator at one of the State Data Centers. We ended up staying in the area for 6 years. We owned a home in Elk Grove. One year I remember our home was on the City Christmas Tour. Rosanna played Christmas Music on her piano as the tour wandered through the house. The Christmas tree that year was outstanding. I think she could have had a whole career as an Interior Decorator.

With her background in Financial Planning – she was a volunteer for the Sacramento Police Department working on Financial Securities Fraud.

The following pages contain pictures of family members.

Pictures

Son Gary and his wife Eunice

Son Gregory

Sister Jan and husband Ted

Sister Cathy and husband Linwood
(Linwood passed away in 2015)

Son Geoff and wife Danielle

As we moved around the state, Rosanna was great at negotiating all my contracts. She also loved to go house shopping. She only looked at new homes, so many were being built at the time. This way she got to select the kitchen tiles, carpeting and wall colors. She was great at adding beautiful furniture and decorations in every home. During the latter part of our marriage we lived in gated communities. This offered more security and Rosanna loved getting involved with the Clubhouse activities. We moved to Desert Hot Springs to a senior gated community called Paradise Springs. We were close to Palm Springs and there was a lot of activity in the Coachella Valley.

When I brought lunches to work everyone wanted to know what I was warming up in the Microwave. Most knew Rosanna and what a great cook she was. They would crowd around and I would announce I'm having Trout Almandine or something like that. Oh boy was I getting spoiled, never ate like this before. My lunches were always great.

The following pages contain pictures of some of our traditional table settings. It also includes pictures taken by guests as we greeted them at the door. This was all part of Rosanna's effort to draw me out as she promised in our wedding vows. I was no longer feeling nerdy or geeky.

Pictures

Rosanna was well known for her Table Settings.
Here are some samples table settings.

In our wedding vows, Rosanna said she would "draw me out" – Oh boy did she ever.

Rosanna loved "theme" dinners. When we had guests for dinner, which was at least twice a month, this is how they were greet at the door. We handed the camera to them to take the picture and it became part of her collection.

Rosanna's son Jay, he was a frequent visitor at our home.

True Love Is Like a Rose

Most flowers in gardens pose,
None more so than the Rose;
Of all the gifts from God above,
None better than to fall I love;
They differ in species and name,
In many ways they are the same;
If both are given thought and care,
Both will blossom in beauty rare.

From tiny bud the Rose will grow,
At first unique and often slow;
We save it from the blossom blight,
Protect it from the insects bite;
From tiny thought love does grow;
With our hearts alike we glow;
We cherish this with all our might,
Protect it so we'll never fight.

Some flowers in gardens pose,
None are scented as the Rose;
Its perfume there does fill the air,
With beauty well beyond compare;
True love also has its effect,
Those far and wide it will infect
With senses filled to overflow,
That everyone can see and know.

Why such beauty with a thorn?
To protect it so it won't be torn;
Or plucked or damaged there,
Just God's way to add some flair?
True love reminds us every day,
To guard those things we often say;

Those thoughts that come out fierce,
There the tender heart does pierce.

Some flowers in gardens pose,
None more so than the Rose;
Of all the gifts from God above,
None more treasured than to love;
Both withstand the winds that blow,
Both with care will grow and grow;
And there for all in fullest sight,
They will glow in brightest light.

Living with Rosanna was always exciting and interesting. I shared in all her activities. A whole new life opened up for me. She was very generous, so willing to help others.

In Sacramento, where she was a member of AAUW (American Association of University Women), assisting them in stocking apartments for newly released female inmates from prison. One in particular interested her. The woman was raped in prison and had a little baby. She came to our home several nights a week as Rosanna went over several school and career choices. Shortly afterwards she enrolled in nursing school which was 4 nights a week. Rosanna asked me, "Do you want to babysit her baby?"

"Yes, it will save her money not having to get someone else." This was the first time we had been around babies together. We had lots of laughs when it came time to feed, bathe and change diapers. This lasted for a while until we moved out of the area. I was always impressed with her finding time to help others, in particular this woman, who was turning her negatives into positives.

As an active member of AAUW Chapters in both Riverside and Palm Springs CA, she was involved with fund raising with her cooking. I joined AAUW as well because I felt it was a worthy cause, and this would support Rosanna in her work. They are instrumental in encouraging young girls to enter the technical or science fields, supported them by sending a group each year for a week at a local campus. The girls were 7th and 8th graders and had been recommended by their teachers. I remember one occasion where the guest speaker was Sally Ride the Astronaut. On another occasion one of the girls went on to become a Micro-Biologist at the Scripps Institute and came back to speak. The girls reported back about their adventure and I was always impressed to see how this encouraged them.

One memorable event occurred while she was President of the Riverside Branch. Riverside has several Sister Cities, one is Sendai Japan. The

AAUW Branch has a special connection to this city involving one of its members who was President at the time. Her son, wounded in Korea, was recovering from his wounds in Sendai. At his request AAUW raised scholarship funds to help several women further their education. Several of them were in the delegation visiting Riverside for the first time that year. The scholarships went on for many years.

For various reasons neither one of us attended church for a long time. We both missed that and what it brought into our lives. One Saturday we visited the Library in downtown Riverside. As we headed back to the car we smelled food cooking as we walked past the back door of a church on the corner. It was the Unitarian Universalist Church of Riverside. We stuck our head in the door and someone in the kitchen invited us in. They were preparing food for after the service the next morning. They asked if we wanted a tour of the church. The church was on a corner close to the Mission Inn. It had been there since the 1800's. Made of red Arizona Sandstone, the inside was beautiful with high ceilings and many stained glass windows.

As we roamed around the church, Rosanna turned to me with tears running down her cheeks, she said "I'm home". I was moved that she was so obviously struck by something within her. We returned the next Sunday for the Service and were even more impressed.

This was the beginning of a long association with this UU church. Rev. Matthew Crary was the Minister. His Sunday Services were always interesting. We saw this church flourish and were so glad to be part of its growth.

There were several things that we loved. They were community oriented. The members were very welcoming, especially regarding the homeless. There were many who congregated around the Library. On Sunday morning the church would serve coffee and refreshments after the service. This was very attractive to them. Many came to the Sunday Service. I remember seeing ushers help them unload and stack their backpacks so they could attend the service, and help them recover their belongings afterwards. I often thought what that one hour of serenity and inspiration must have meant to them.

In addition, the City of Riverside held a homeless event every year. They would close off some city streets for this; the church was within this zone. Here the homeless would be treated to free showers, haircuts and to personal counselling. This also included physical and dental exams as well as job opportunities. It was very impressive. The church would open its doors and serve lunch during this time.

(We dined by candlelight often, it is truly magical)

The Magic of the Candle

I want the magic of the candle to dwell within my home,
To scare away the demons wherever they may roam;
Shining in darkened corners and all hidden places,
Exposing scary and often frightening faces.

I want the magic of the candle to dwell where we dine
I want to see light filtered through my glass of wine;
I want to see the candlelight dancing in your eyes,
I want to hear your happiness in a million sighs.

There is no history here, no need to bring the past,
The candle will ensure us that love alone will last;
We will always bask in the healing of the light,
The magic of the candle helps us through the night.

I want the magic of the candle to dwell where I abide,
It will be our reminder that once you were my bride;
I want love and happiness reflected in the light,
Listening to the music we will dance away the night.

*(We used candles often around the house; there is
something comforting about this special light)*

After several years we moved to Desert Hot Springs, near Palm Springs. We attended the UU church in Rancho Mirage. Rev. Ken MacLean was the Minister and we enjoyed his sermons. They had a theatrical group in the church and were also involved with a homeless program. Rosanna and I became actively involved with all their interests and Rosanna was involved heavily in the cooking for special occasions

They had an Annual Auction where members would put up items for bidding. Rosanna would offer several dinners at our house, such as Prime Rib. The members would bid on seats at the table. I remember one occasion the seats going for $55 a seat and we served eight. It was a great way to raise funds and Rosanna loved the cooking. We would purchase the food - that was our donation; the funds would go to the church. Rosanna would prepare the center-piece for the table and one place setting. I would then prepare the rest of the settings, clear the table and wash them all later. During the meal I would sit at the table participating in the conversation. Rosanna would prepare each plate and deliver them to the table. What a team! After the meal she would entertain on her piano.

Rosanna was involved with many of the church activities. One activity, in particular was Thanksgiving. On that day the church opened its doors and we had many members participate. Most had no family in the area. This was their family. They were invited to include guests. Rosanna would start cooking a Turkey and Ham at home and then bring them to church to continue cooking. We attended every year we were there a very memorable event.

One day she received a call from my son Geoff. Unknown to me, Geoff had been heavily involved with drugs. He needed to go through Drug Rehabilitation. She was willing to pay for this. I was so proud of her and so relieved that I didn't know about this, because I would have worried. After rehab, he helped his friend Danielle end her addiction. Shortly after this they were married; Rosanna and I attended the wedding. They have now been married over 10 years and totally free of drugs during that entire time. Every Sunday they both go to Narcotics Anonymous Meetings to help others fight this problem. They have turned a negative into a positive. Am I proud of them both? You bet!

During this period I traveled 70 miles to work. I would leave early Monday, stay in the area 4 nights and return on Friday after work. One of the places I stayed was a home we had for sale in Riverside. It was only 15 minutes from work. I told her one day that I missed her when I was away during the week, even though we talked on the phone every evening.

Each week when I left I would have things to take to the other house for the week. When I arrived I started to unpack, on the bottom of the bag was a box with Rosanna's picture on it. When I opened it I laughed, the inside was filled with her hair. She had been losing hair over a period and was saving it to have a fall made or something of that sort. When I talked to her on the phone that night she asked, "Did you find the box?" I confirmed that I found it. She said, "It's for those occasions when you miss me". We laughed over this for a long time. I called it my "Rosanna box".

During this period we flourished in our marriage. We also grew individually. This was the most productive period of my entire career. Rosanna was sought after by every group we belonged. I would say these were the happiest times. There is something about getting involved. It brings out the best in you, especially those you interact with in the community. Everyone benefits.

Rosanna's son Jay was a frequent guest. On occasion he had electrical contracts in the area. Rosanna loved cooking for him, I'm sure he loved it as well. We visited him when he moved to Coos Bay, Oregon. She loved all the greenery.

(I told her often how much I loved her; there are no limits in my mind)

I Love You More

I love you more than heaven's garment hem can reach,
More than all the grains of sand upon the beach;
I love you more than there are mountains here to climb,
More than all the clocks that, measure endless time;
I love you more each time you speak my name,
Or hear your voice, now even music's not the same;
I love you more each time I look into your eyes,
I see into the very depths of where love lies;
I love you more each time I feel your touch,
Just to hold your hand, to me, means so much.

I love you more each time I smell your hair,
It fills my senses with something beyond compare;
I love you more than words can possibly express,
More than all the stars in heaven we could guess;
I love you more each time we kiss good-night,
You take away my breath, darkness becomes light;
I love you more each passing day when you are near,
The hours seem like weeks when you're not here;
I love you more than I could possibly confess,
I do not think that I could ever love you less.

(Just as the stars, this love is for eternity)

We were able to take occasional vacations. There were cruises to Alaska and to Hawaii.

Rosanna loved to surprise me. We flew to Jamaica on one of my Birthdays. The morning we were flying out she said, "Why don't you take the luggage outside and wait for the shuttle, they should be here shortly." I said, "Okay". I dragged everything outside and waited. Around the corner came the longest Limousine I've ever seen. The driver got out and said, "Happy Birthday Mr. Parent". I turned around to look at the house and Rosanna was standing in the window with the biggest grin on her face. What a memorable occasion. Everyone needs to take a Limo ride at least once in their life.

On our cruise to Alaska, we docked and took a helicopter ride up to a glacier for a ride in dog sleds.

There were 6 couples. The women sat in the sled and the guys rode the back as a musher. Rosanna said, "I want to drive", so I said, "OK" I then sat in the sled and Rosanna mushed. Everyone thought this was great, we laughed about this for years. This was classic Rosanna!!

Life was going great. I loved working as long as I could. It was very satisfying to accomplish some of the hurdles that faced the companies I worked for. I'm still in touch today with many of my co-workers.

On my way home each Friday after being away all week, I would pull into a rest area to call Rosanna, to let her know I would be there within the hour. When I arrived home, after the usual warm greeting, I would sit where she had poured a glass of my favorite Chardonnay. She would then sit at her Ivory Baby Grand piano and play my favorite - Beethoven's "Fur Elise." In my mind, this was as close to heaven as I could imagine. In my final hours on earth, I will think back to this time, hear that wonderful music, smell Rosanna's perfume and feel the love.

Chapter 5 Summary
Some comments to help you turn some of these negatives into positives.

1. **Partnering**. In my first marriage, this was the norm, but over the years this has changed. Marriage is my preference rather than any other arrangement. I needed commitment not anything temporary or living together even for a short period. Whatever the arrangement, you are in, they all have one factor in common – love. It's important to love, appreciate and help each other.

2. **Family Members**. Meeting your loved ones family members. Keep an open mind and don't be judgmental, hopefully they will be the same toward you. Remember, these are the same family members who will be there for you in your time of need. This also goes the other way – you may need to step up and help them in a time of need. This is what family life is all about. We turn negatives into positives.

3. **Support each other**. Be prepared for new and different things in each other's life. Participate together initially, it may grow on you. If this turns out to not work, find a way to spend time apart doing something different, but be supportive. Don't try to force change. Rosanna was more active than I was, but I found ways to support her in her endeavors. She belonged to several book clubs and enjoyed that activity. I would always find something to do out of the house to give her the time she needed.

4. **Maintain your love**. Love your partner through thick and thin. Be there for each other. It may be a health issue or some past issue that keeps popping up. Some health issues may be long standing. You can even help support others in the same predicament. Turn a negative into a positive.

5. **Forgiveness.** One is forgiving others and the other is forgiveness of debts
   (a) **(Others**. So someone did or said something stupid. Do you really want that to harden your heart? Do you really want that to drag on through your entire life? Do you really want

that to stand in the way of the blessings that lay ahead? Take care of it, life is too short, turn that negative into a positive

(b) **Debts**. If a family member borrowed money or did something that hasn't been repaid. Find a way to resolve it. Maybe have them do something for you then call it squared away. Don't let it ferment over time. Rosanna was so generous. Not only did she help my son Geoff when he needed funds for Drug Rehabilitation, she helped my other two sons in their time of need as well. So should I get all uptight about who paid her back or not? **NO**. The bottom line is the results. The fact that Geoff and his wife Danielle not only turned their life around, but spend each Sunday helping others do the same is far more payment that I could ever receive. They have turned a negative into a positive and are helping others do the same

6. **Active as a couple**. Be involved together in some outside activities. This gets you out of the house, maybe even your comfort zone. You will interact with others. This outside connection is important. These are also people who will be supportive when the need arises. You are sowing seeds now that you will be able to harvest later.

7. **Leisure time**. Spend time together away now and then. Even a weekend can be important. By loving each other you will continue to love the different things you learn about each other. Oh, maybe something you don't like about your partner? Intelligently handle these, be supportive and gracefully turn any negatives into positives. Rosanna and I voted differently, at the polls we would cancel each other out. But, when it came to those other items on the ballot we sometimes wouldn't see eye to eye. We spent lots of time discussing the merits on both sides. There were times when we actually got the other to change their mind. But we never yelled or shouted each other down. We handled it intelligently

8. **Retirement**. Rosanna retired before I did. It depends on so many factors. Remember you are moving into a fixed income

unless you have some investments to help. I loved work, it allowed me to interact with people, and I loved solving problems throughout my entire career. I think retirement for any couple really takes planning. You have expenses if you travel and if you want to remain active, I would suggest phasing into it as much as possible. If you work for a large company ask if you can work 1 or 2 days a week on orienting new employees. Here you have years of experience and can guide new people through the email protocols and online activities allowed at work. Also, many people when they retire, now find they are home and this can take some adjusting to be together all day, all evening too. You may want to find some outside activity to get involved with. When I retired and was underfoot at home, Rosanna would gather some coupons she saved for gourmet spices to be used in her cooking and send me out to find them. I would be gone for hours, may even have to go to several places. But I had time to get coffee and she was able to work on eBay, create recipes or menus. It was a win-win for both of us.

9. **Prior partners**. If one or both of you were married or had partners before, be sure to handle any negatives. These could be children during that marriage or other issues. Having someone new in your life is great, let others see and feel this love as well. It is never too late to correct things done in the past. Now is the time to help turn negatives into positives. Help your loved one do the same.

10. **Your comfort zone**. I was proud to be one of the few males in our AAUW Chapter. How inspiring to see them encourage girls to enter the fields where they are not highly represented. There were very few men to talk to, but as you will see in Chapter 7, these were the people who helped support me later.

11. **Treasure Chest**. This is where you keep all those treasured moments. Keep filling it; this is where you return to refresh your memories about the wonderful life spent with your loved one. Hopefully as you remain together and keep adding your life's moments, you will keep saying "It's not big enough".

CHAPTER 6

Losing Rosanna

Closing Doors

Something about a closing door,
That seems so final, so complete;
It seems at times a deafening roar,
Of heartbreak and departing feet.

Something about a closing door,
Like trying to shut something out;
Perhaps the door closed before,
Its finality could be in doubt.

Something about a closing door,
It can't always be so bad;
It can at times make feelings soar,
Or once again a heart that's glad.

Something about a closing door,
It gives us a chance to review;
Before we say, let's hear it no more,
Perhaps the start of something new.

It started with pain in the lower abdomen. Rosanna hated pain. She tried using whatever medication she had for pain. It wasn't working. We called 911. She was taken to Desert Regional Hospital. She was there for several days while they ran tests and got the pain under control. She was then transferred to a rehab center until they could get her stabilized with the new medications.

I visited the rehab center twice daily. I worried about her. She returned home after about four days and was able to sleep as she followed up with a specialist for further testing.

We went together to her doctor to get the results. He said, "Rosanna you have Ovarian Cancer". She asked, "How bad is it? "He said, "Its terminal, but they are doing amazing things with Chemo these days". She asked him to describe the treatment and length of time. As he talked, I could tell from the look on her face she wasn't going to go for Chemo treatment and the consequences. She then asked, "How long if no Chemo"? He said, "Two months max" He suggested we get a second opinion.

It was a long, quiet ride home.

How could this be happening again? It's like
being struck by lightning twice.

I was in panic mode again. Rosanna handled everything from banking, taxes and investing. We even had a home in Riverside for sale, she was handling everything. She was trying to get our current mortgage reworked.

We contacted people to get a second opinion. The appointments were made and we waited for the date.

I called her son, Jay, to let him know. He talked to her several times. I called my sister Jan.

Friends and neighbors were calling; some saw the ambulance and she missed several book club meetings. When I answered the phone, I checked to see if she wanted to talk to anyone. The answer was no for now. I told everyone we were still reviewing our situation. We had long talks on how we would handle this.

The date arrived to get the second opinion. First came the testing then the meeting for the results. I attended with her. The doctor knew this was a second opinion, he was upbeat for her. The results were the same. He recommended that we try Chemo. We thanked him. The second opinion was sent to our Primary Doctor.

She clearly didn't want Chemo. We agreed that we wanted to remain at home and call a hospice group. We also decided to tell friends, relatives and neighbors what was going on.

Initially there were knocks on the door, people wanting to talk to her and lots of phone calls. Then they respected our privacy.

We had a celebrity neighbor who was on television for a number of years. She loved Rosanna and came to see her before going on an engagement for a short while. I remember them sitting on the couch together talking and laughing. She was so upbeat and told Rosanna when she left that she would beat this.

The final weeks

I was unable to go to work and I worried all the time. She put on a brave face. The days that followed were not happy days. She was going downhill fast. We contacted Family Hospice Care. Memories returned and I recalled being so worn out caring for Virginia with the lack of sleep. I was looking forward to hearing what was available to us through hospice care.

The Family Hospice Care came by to talk to us. We agreed they could help and signed on. The agreement was that they would provide all services, treatments, medical supplies, equipment and medications. They would come on a regular basis and when called.

The hospital bed and equipment arrived the next day and was set up in the living room. Her piano, used several times a week was pushed into the corner. The house was taking on a sense of urgency. Doctors and nurses would be arriving all hours of the day and night as needed. Most of them came by to introduce themselves, all well experienced. The group provided me with a list of food to keep handy as well as space needed in the fridge for medication. I was given numbers to call at any time.

I walked around the house trying to determine what normal was going to be. The dining room table was set for guests, a dinner that had to be cancelled. I kept in touch with my co-workers; some of them had been to our home. Family members were kept posted several times a week. I needed to be sure the house was quiet so she could rest. Some neighbors came by wanting to see her and offering encouragement, but I had to refuse to let them in and stepped outside to talk with them. Church members called to offer any assistance as well as members of AAUW. She was dearly loved by all.

She talked to her son Jay; he was unable to visit because of a project underway.

I tried to maintain a happy, hopeful face, but I had been here before. We had only weeks.

The brightest light of my life was about to go out.
...Oh no not again, I quietly cried.

You came into my life one day and it's never been the same,
....now you'll be leaving me....

The visits began from Hospice Care, both doctor and nurses. I had a list of medications to give her at appointed times. This went on day and night. Rosanna loved the people that came. They were so upbeat, friendly and very professional. There was even humor; I loved to hear her laugh.

She slept a lot, probably the medications. I was standing by her side at one point, when she opened her eyes. She said, "So this is it?" I held her hand and cried silently. I felt so helpless.

As Rosanna was slipping away, I would walk the house in the dark not wanting to turn on lights and disturb her sleep. But, there was another reason – I couldn't bear to see all of the beauty she created in our home. The dining room table was set to entertain guests. Everywhere I looked was Rosanna's touch of beauty – keeping the lights off, helped me cope with this.

One evening, late at night – I walked the house. As I stood looking out from her office at the moon-lit backyard, I had reached my lowest point.

My cell phone rang – it was my son Geoff, inquiring about Rosanna and informing me that he had wonderful news. He said, "Danielle is expecting" I said, "But how? I thought she was told she could never have children". This would be their first child, my first grandchild. To hear the excitement and happiness in his voice was overwhelming. I tried to express my joy for him while sobbing – I'm not sure he even understood a word I said. The range of emotion at that moment was so extreme.

After the call I remember Danielle calling me about a dream she had about Virginia. My God it was coming true!

When Rosanna was awake I told her. She was happy for them and said "Oh boy they will have their hands full."

> .... Something about a closing door,
> .....That seems so final, so complete;

It has been written "As one door closes…another opens." I felt this was God's way of telling me not to give up, there are other things going on here. I also believe it was the results of many friends who were praying and keeping good thoughts for us both, I truly felt uplifted and loved at that moment.

The television was silenced, the rooms were dark. I wandered aimlessly around the house. I needed to be quiet, I needed time to think and not worry. There were very few phone calls; I was so thankful that everyone understood.

One night the phone rang. It was Rev. Ken MacLean from our church (UUCOD). He was on vacation in London. I was overwhelmed with emotion and couldn't talk, but I told him I would listen. His kind words of encouragement even from that distance gave me strength to go on. It lasted only a few moments. But I so much appreciated him calling, tending to his flock while on vacation. I will always remember that moment. It is the little things in life that mean so much.

The final days

Hospice Care was continually visiting day and night. Members of the team included the physician who was the medical director, an RN Case Manager who was coordinating the support given also Health Aides tending to bathing and personal care. One would write a report and go over it with me before leaving.

On Wednesday, Rosanna's son Jay called and said he would be flying down on Monday. I was so glad; Rosanna would be pleased to see him. He talked to her on the phone.

The Hospice Care nurse called to ask if everything was alright. Giving me some things to watch for when the end would be near. There was such calmness in her voice. I made notes, hoping it would never come. This group was so professional; they knew everything and had so much experience. I was so glad they were available. I thought back to Virginia's passing. I sure could have used something like this.

The lights were still off; I lit candles to give some light. We had lots of candles and used them often.

> ….*I want to see the candlelight dancing in your eyes…*
> … *I want to hear your happiness in a million sighs….*

> ….*Oh God…The candlelight was no longer dancing in her eyes,*
> ….*I no longer hear her happy sighs*

On Friday, the day was so long. Late afternoon I went into her office to look out into the back yard. I saw a rabbit near the window. We've had them in the yard before; they usually hop around looking for green shoots out of the ground to munch on. This one was not moving around, he was in the shade under a bush.

On Saturday morning, I received a call from Hospice Care, they read the doctors report. She again gave me a number to call if there were signs indicating the end was nearing. I wrote it down. Since I was in the office I looked out the window again and there was the same rabbit. Still not hopping around or eating but had moved to a different shrub for the shade.

During the day, on Saturday I made sure Rosanna was comfortable and gave her the medication at the prescribed times. Someone from Hospice Care came by to tend to her needs in the late afternoon. While she was there I returned to the office. The rabbit was still in the yard, still not eating or hopping around, but I saw it had moved to a different shrub. I thought, how strange, to hang around this long, it was like it was on duty. Like there was a purpose to the visit.

During Saturday evening I remained quiet, so she could sleep. I sat nearby dozing in a chair. When I woke it was after midnight. I checked on her and she was exhibiting the behavior I was told to call them about.

When I called from the office, the person was so calm. We continued talking; she stayed on the line with me. I laid the phone down several times and went in to check on her. I performed what I was instructed to do each time, such as holding a mirror under her nose. She was less responsive and had shallow breathing.

Finally it was over. She was no longer breathing. They would send the doctor over immediately to confirm and fill out the necessary paperwork. I called a pre-arranged number to have her picked up after the doctor left. I gave the papers to the people and she was removed in the wee hours of the morning to be cremated.

My darling girl was gone. I was alone with God, just as before.

I love you more than heaven's garment hem can reach
… Oh God….please keep her close by

I sat at the kitchen dining area table and sobbed. I fell asleep there near her kitchen, her favorite room in the house.

When I woke I was slumped over the kitchen table. It was getting light out, but still too early to call Jay to tell him the sad news. I looked across the room at her piano, pushed aside into the corner and the bed, now empty. The writing tablet under where I fell asleep was wet from my tears. I had written something before falling asleep.

I kissed your brow a final time before you slipped away,
I hope you were aware, I prayed that you would stay;
I told you that I loved you; I hoped that you would hear,
I held your hand; did you sense that I was near?

We were alone in that final moment, you and I,
We would not want it any other way to say goodbye;
We'll meet once again, you and I, in a better place,
I cherish the time we had and look to that embrace.

I went to the office to get ready to call Jay and other family members. I need to begin working on an Obituary so everyone would know. I looked out the back window, to search the yard for the rabbit. It was gone, I never saw it again.

I had so much on my plate. I worried about access to her accounts, the home for sale in Riverside, the taxes coming up at year end. It was overwhelming.

I finally contacted Jay. We talked for a few minutes; he would be arriving on Monday. I called my sister Jan and told her the news. I told her about the rabbit that stayed for a few days in the backyard. She said she would email be information from Steven Farmers book, "Animal Spirit Guides"

I called several people that needed to know, and then started gathering information for her obituary. I was glad Jay was coming he could help me fill in some of the blanks.

It was Sunday, the same day Virginia died, and it was the same month, September.

.....remember the Sabbath Day...oh God...I
will...I will...I will never forget

(In my anguish, I had to ask)

Why Her, Why Now?

Lord, I'll not question your wisdom,
Nor your words to deny or disavow;
But this one thing I can't comprehend,
Not remotely. Why her? Why now?

If you needed her by your side,
What event could not wait?
Could I not have a decade more?
A small amount, can't she be late?

Why her? Could you not have found
A substitute, a stand-in, an alternate?
Could you not find someone else?
Not even change the date?

I'm now beginning to understand,
You see her as we do, and need her now
Unique and irreplaceable as she is;
Now I understand; why her, why now.

(I'm sure this has been asked before my many others)

In an hour or so I got an email from Jan regarding the rabbit. It was a copy of a page from Steven Farmers Book "Animal Spirit Guides".

Here's what jumped out at me:

> *If a rabbit shows up –*
> - *This is a very creative time for you, so it's important to quickly take advantage of any opportunity that comes your way unexpectedly*
> - *You're going to find yourself going through a period of quiet and stillness followed by a burst of intense activity*
> - *Rather than steady, step by-step progress you'll see it happen in leaps and bounds*

I received a dinner invitation from my next door neighbor. Marsha and Cleo had been so kind. As we talked over dinner I mentioned that I had so much on my plate including the taxes and home for sale in Riverside. She asked, "Do you know Henry up the street/? He does taxes"

I admitted I did not. I left for home after dinner, I had lots to do. About half an hour after arriving home, there was a knock on the door. Henry Broussard, a neighbor introduced himself. We walked to the kitchen and talked. I told him what I had ahead of me. The upcoming taxes; the home for sale, also having to continue with Rosanna's effort to get our mortgage rewritten. We talked for a short while. He offered to do the taxes and once sold real estate so he could answer any questions. He also would put me in touch with a facilitator who works with banks on getting mortgages reworked. In five minutes he had taken all of the items off my plate. This was unreal. I couldn't believe that the rabbit promise was being fulfilled.

Rosanna's son, Jay, arrived on Monday. He felt terrible that he missed seeing his mother. He did talk with her on the phone. He was a frequent visitor to our home over the years and they talked often.

My immediate problem was to get her passwords for the computer and be able to use the online banking to pay bills. I had automatic deposit so the money would be there. Rosanna did so much, I felt overwhelmed. She was so organized. I searched around her computer and found where she kept all the Logon information and the associated Passwords. Jay logged on to the banking system and walked me through the online banking steps. Fortunately for me, he used the same bank and used the same system. As we looked at the account he said, "Look at this", I leaned closer to see the details. "Here's a bill she paid just a week ago". I do remember hearing her get up and go into the office on occasion, she was not totally bed-ridden. But this also shows how quickly she had gone downhill.

The next order of business was to get an Obituary into the local paper. He was able to get the necessary information and I had a current picture that was not very good, but we used it anyway. The Obituary was in the paper on Wednesday.

Before Jay left to go home I had several things to do. One was to pick up her ashes after the cremation. Rosanna requested there be no service and wanted her ashes scattered in Oregon. We had been there a couple of times to visit Jay and she just loved it.

We drove to where she was cremated. Jay drove me home. I had her remains in my lap. It was a quiet ride. I had both hands on the box with her final remains, tears rolling down my cheeks.

> ....*I love you more each passing day when you are near.....*
> ....*The hours seem like weeks when you're not here.....*
> ....*I love you more than I could possibly confess......*
> ....*I do not think that I could ever love you less.*

Rosanna and I did not have time to get a Will updated, so I opted for a Living Trust using LegalZoom. I filled out information online, the bank address and account numbers. There were also pages for investment information, mortgage and any other assets. I also filled out current addresses for my three sons and named one as the executor. I also provided information on how any assets will be distributed later. In addition there were forms for my Health Care Directive and also for my final wishes. Once completed online, I received the total package in two days with directions on which pages that needed to be notarized and witnessed.

Before the week was over I had a call from the president of our church. He asked if we could have a Memorial Service for Rosanna, so many people had been asking and all loved her. Thinking back to the dinner for Virginia, I remembered several people telling me that it was not enough closure for them. I agreed and a date was set. I notified people I thought should know.

I drove Jay to the airport. He was such a big help. I told him I would be in touch so I could visit Oregon to scatter his mother's ashes.

Grief Counseling was available through my Health Plan and the hospital. I felt comfortable and strong. I knew I would be alright since I had earlier found that rock I knew was within me when Virginia passed away. This time there was no thoughts of suicide. I felt strong.

Our celebrity neighbor returned from her engagement and knocked on the door. She had been away only six weeks. I told her the news, she was so sad. I watched her as she walked back to her home, her head down.

During the night after her passing, I would hear her calling me, "Erwin, Erwin"

> *I would jump out of bed and rush out to the living room, saying "I'm here, I'm here". I would even check the other rooms hoping she was there. This lasted for several weeks.*

Once awake it was difficult for me to get back to sleep. While she was ill there was a lot of activity, people coming and going at all hours of the day and night. Now there was only quiet, a stillness almost unbearable. I would often sit and cry over the loss of such a dear wife. I needed to find a way to move on, as I did before.

...Oh Lord help me, please bring her back.

(I'm always impressed by the devotion of many to honor those buried)

Bouquets

Flowers are God's gift to man,
Some grow on vines others stand;
Every form and shape and hue,
In fields, mountains, oceans too;
Some unseen in darkest places,
Some droop or have upturned faces.

We use them in many diverse ways,
It sometimes replaces words to say;
Weddings, funerals, in the hair,
Gifts to teachers, for those who care;
To a Veteran from a grateful nation,
A single, solemn white Carnation.

I will bring you bouquets every day,
No need for me to find words to say;
Each flower has meaning of its own,
Each flower loved where it was grown;
This will express my love for you,
I will bring you bouquets, not a few.

So, when your days are ended here,
This is a reminder that I'm still near;
I will gather flowers where they grow,
Find them on hillsides where they glow;
I will bring you bouquets every day
And place them gently where you lay.

(Rosanna loved flowers; she grew them in her garden
and used them in our home and our dining table)

Chapter 6 Summary
Some comments to help you turn some of these negatives into positives.

1. **Bitterness**. How easy it would be for me to be bitter. I lost two wonderful wives in a short time the same way. Both died on a Sunday in September. What was prominent for me was not the tragedy but the blessings they brought to my life. I refused to let this harden my heart or to block my view of the goodness happening around me. I was adamant that I was going to somehow turn this negative into a positive. You should seek those close to you, whether a relative, a friend, or someone from your religion. Find ways to seek comfort.

2. **Home care**. Having cared for Virginia with my sister, I found it was extremely tiring. I think hospice care is so great. They are so professional, knowledgeable and caring. Please look into this service. There is no place like being at home. In my case it was short term. For prolonged health issues seek guidance from the health professionals in your area or your Health Plan. This is constantly changing. Being at home is less expensive than a care facility and there are so many caretakers now available. It could be a blessing for both you and your loved one. I vowed to both Virginia and Rosanna that they would not die among strangers. I was alone with both of them in the end. I cherish those final minutes. Think of the many who never had this opportunity and wish they did. Another thing I loved about Family Hospice Care, they followed up with me, calling every few months to see how I was doing, if I was moving ahead.

3. **Animals**. If there were animals present I would suggest looking into Steven Farmer's book, "Animal Spirit Guides". The book has over 200 animals. It will give you insight into what it may mean. For me, the rabbit was noticeable. When I talked to friends, some did see an animal; it looked out of place and was acting unusual. Also, Pat Spork's book about "Animal Sightings" has some inspiring stories.

In these final moments, I felt that I was also her guide. Think back to when your children started school. You held them by the hand and escorted them to school and probably said, "It will be alright, I'll be right here; they will take good care of you." Or when your children married, you handed them over to someone else. There was deep trust. So here we have a sad and painful moment,

*I held her hand.…..It will be alright, I'll be right
here, they will take good care of you…*

4. **Planning.** Involve your family members in any major decisions regarding your house and your future plans. They only want the best for you. In fact, they may have some helpful ideas. If necessary have a family meeting and discuss all the options. This isn't an easy decision, it may take several meetings. Be inspired. What can you do that would please your loved one. Listen to any interesting ideas they have.

5. **Living Trust**. I used a well know company they are available online. I found them to be reputable and clear on what was needed. I have since gone out and updated pages several times. You might want to discuss this with family so that everyone is on the same page.

6. **Friends**. Don't hibernate; treasure your close friends and family members. They will be there for you in this time of need. With Virginia's passing I felt the need to be alone, I needed to find that rock I knew was somewhere within me. I think having people around me all the time would have prevented me or prolonged my search. But with Rosanna's passing I loved all the friends around me. They were my "Angels." Find your own comfort level.

7. **Grief Counseling**. I encourage anyone who needs support to look into this. It is usually available to you through the hospitals or your health plan.

I have a friend, Carolyn, who went through grief counseling after losing her husband Ralph.

Here are her comments.

Nobody can really relate who has not experienced the loss of a spouse. In the group you receive understanding and compassion without judgment or attempt to give you a quick fix, or a Band-Aid, or things that are not really helpful You realize that you are not alone, and that you are not the only one going through this experience The group is a safe place to feel and express your grief. The facilitator offers helpful facts about the grieving process, including that it is an individual process and to not compare your experience to another's. In grief counseling one receives empathy reassurance and support.

Personally, I do not see any negatives to grief counseling and grief support groups. To me support groups are helpful whatever they are for. I find that nothing can compare to one person who is having a particular problem reaching out to another who is facing the same problem. When I am at a support group I see God in action, working through individuals and it is profound.

My experience has been positive. I know there are others who have different views but you will have to find them to get those views. Groups work for me and I'm grateful they do.

8. **Suicide**. With Virginia's death the thought lasted two days. It never happened with Rosanna. I will cover what happened and why in the next chapter. If you have thoughts of suicide please discuss this with someone close to you. Here is the National Suicide Prevention Hot Line 1-800-273-8255. With Virginia,

if I had followed through with this thought, think of what I would have missed:

- meeting Rosanna and having a wonderful 17 year marriage
- at age 76, looking into the beautiful face of my first grand-child, Virginia Rosanna Parent.

Don't cut your future short, you have life after this death, your loved one would want you to carry on. Make them proud, be inspired

9. **Treasure Chest** Keep your treasure chest handy. All those wonderful memories, pictures and special moments. These will begin to come into prominence as you prepare to move ahead

10. **Talk to your loved one.** I talk to Virginia and Rosanna. I don't always watch the "Long Island Medium" on television, but she constantly tells her clients – "Talk to them. They are right here". I talk to both Virginia and Rosanna in low whispers while walking, before I sleep and when I wake up. You may never get a verbal response, but it may be helpful information sent to you in some other way. I discuss this in Chapter 8.

11. **Dreams**. Pay attention to your dreams. Remember I wrote a poem based on a dream. Never reject the idea that you won't be contacted by this method. In Chapter 8 I share some experiences by family members. One dream was 19 years after Virginia's passing and by someone who never met her. Have you had any experiences similar to this?

12. **Expect the unexpected**. Expect to be contacted in some way. I mention in Chapter 8 several experiences. One that involves a shopping list and a Valentine's Day card left early morning at work in a highly secure office.

13. **Be inspired**. I love the story of John Wooden, the famous UCLA Basketball Coach. When his wife died after 53 years of marriage, he left a letter on her pillow every night.

Think of what you can do. Reach for inspiration and ideas. Turn negatives into positives.

14. **Try Writing**. I always loved poetry, so that was my means of sharing my feelings. I never dreamed I would write a book and now I have so many more ideas to write even more. The blessings you receive will be endless.

CHAPTER 7

Harvesting the Seeds Sown as a Couple

The obituary was published in the Desert Sun Newspaper on Wednesday. The harvesting began almost immediately. The phone kept ringing and there were people at the front door.

During our years of marriage, Rosanna and I had been involved with so many things together. Some were AAUW events or Clubhouse events or church events. She was so talented and capable. All those years we were sowing the seeds of good. Now that she was gone I began reaping all those good works. The Treasure Chest, filled over the years to overflowing was now providing me with friends and activities to keep me busy.

There were no thoughts this time of suicide. This time I was too busy, too active, too involved. I was surrounded by love.

There was a knock on the door. One of the AAUW members gave me a picture of Rosanna that was taken just weeks before. It was the best I had ever seen. It's the one used in this book and is also used on her Facebook page (Dining with Rosanna – which is still in use today).

This was followed by invitations from friends, neighbors, church members and AAUW members for lunch or dinner. I was so grateful to be able to get out of the house. This went on for several years.

My neighbor Henry was always available when I had questions or needed assistance with any personal matter. Just think, he lived only 5 or 6 houses up the street and I didn't meet him until after Rosanna passed away. To me this was more than special. I will never forget the help and support he gave me.

The date arrived for her Memorial Service. It was held at UUCOD (Unitarian/Universalist Church of The Desert) in Rancho Mirage where we were members. My son Geoff came down with his family. Rosanna's son Jay attended. My sister Jan and her husband Ted also attended. The church was filled with friends, neighbors, AAUW members and church members. Some of her friends traveled down from the Sacramento area.

The Minister, Rev. MacLean conducted the service. Rev. Crary from Riverside also spoke. I was too overwhelmed to speak. To hear those attending with their kind words about Rosanna was just too much for me to handle. Rosanna's son Jay spoke about his mother. My poem "You", written for Rosanna, was read by Rev. Maclean.

After her passing I became more active in AAUW serving as their Public Policy Contact, providing information for their monthly newsletter. They also had "Zip Code Luncheons". This is for members living in the same zip code to attend luncheons in between our regular monthly meetings. It was helpful to be around friends and talk about the latest movies or vacation trips.

I also became more involved in church, serving on the Board of Directors and many other activities.

Finally It was time for me to go to scatter her ashes in Oregon. I contacted Jay and set a date. I planned to stay with him a few days. There were two places that she loved when we visited.

One was the Deans Creek Elk viewing area. Rosanna would never visit zoos; she hated to see animals caged. Here the elk roamed the area in this natural environment. When we visited they passed close to where we parked. We sat there for a while as they walked past us just a few feet away. She said "How beautiful to see them up close and totally calm." I can still see the look on her face. I took her ashes and wandered along the path where they walked.

> ....*Ashes and tears fall to the ground,*
> .... *Prayers and love upward bound.*

We then drove to the second area. It was a bluff overlooking the Pacific Ocean off the Cape Arago Highway. It was a beautiful day and the view was spectacular. She and I stood there awhile admiring the view and holding hands. Today it was even more beautiful. I walked slowly along the bluff scattering her ashes.

>........*Ashes and tears fall to the ground,*
>........*Prayers and love upward bound.*

I had fulfilled her final wishes. I then headed home. I needed to get back to work.

(Remembering the trauma I had, having to cut off Virginia's ring)

My Wedding Ring

It circles my heart, makes me complete,
I cherish happy times it brought to me;
How proud I was to be your spouse,
I think that I will wear it for eternity.

It is endless, as memories I have of you,
Some may have faded but are still there;
You placed it on my finger long ago,
To remove it now, a thought I cannot bear.

It's as solid and complete as our marriage
The ups and downs we shared with courage;
It was a magnificent brave adventure,
Thank you for sharing this happy voyage.

It is unbroken and strong like our vows,
The words we wrote and taken deeply;
Words uttered cannot be taken back,
I think that I will wear it for eternity.

When I arrived home in the desert it had been raining. As I exited the freeway to drive up to our gated community there was a double rainbow across the sky. When I got closer to the gate I noticed one end of the inner rainbow was on our house. This was an omen to me. I felt very special and truly blessed.

Once in the house I toured the back yard and noticed that her plants needed water. They were in large pots that were on wheels. Before I left, I dragged all the pots together under the patio cover in the shade so I could get them watered using a timer while I was gone.

When I returned to work I found everyone so sympathetic about Rosanna's passing. It was the hugs without words that meant so much. Those who loved her as I did made me feel real special. I will be forever grateful for the employees of Southern California Edison.

One in particular, Rob, was now remarried; his first wife passed from a brain tumor, his second wife was killed in an auto accident on the way to work. He never got to say goodbye. We talked a lot. Rob is an employee of Southern California Edison where I contracted for 7 years. At this point, I was toying with the idea of creating a DVD with all of Rosanna's recipes. I started scanning them and found some software that could be used to put all this together. Rob was very technical, so one day I asked if he would help, explaining that perhaps he could find some closure in this effort. He agreed and this began a long effort of going to his house once or twice a week to make it happen. I will be forever indebted to him for doing this with me. His wife and young step-daughter made me so welcome. It was finally completed and he gave me two copies. One was sent to Washington DC for Copyright Approval. This was received about a year later. Due to lack of funding the DVD was never produced.

Each weekend when I returned home I found the plants needed more than water. It was Rosanna's TLC they missed. As a city kid, I saw very few flowers around. I was green thumb-less, I felt so helpless. I asked neighbors and friends if they would take them off my hands. All the plants that Rosanna loved and used in her food preparation were now dying. For me it was like death by a thousand cuts.

For some reason the DVD with her recipes was not enough. I followed through with the idea of putting up a Website. www.diningwithrosanna. com was launched. It was supported by family members. The website host made it easy for me to update on a monthly basis. We uploaded seasonal recipes and table settings, so they could be downloaded for free. Family members also wrote articles and presented recipes as well.

This web-site was my Taj Mahal. It gave me an opportunity to tell the world about her. But there was another reason. This was one way to keep her alive. Keep her in my life, keep her relevant. It almost became an obsession. The site was up and available for 3 years. It was getting costly.

Each week I was able to look at the website stats to see who was looking and what pages were the most popular. I started documenting and found that the visitors included 5 of the 7 continents and every major country in each. One month there were over 2,600 hits. People from Europe, Russia, the UK. Also, most South American countries; Canada, Japan, Korea, China, the Philippines, Australia and New Zealand. It went on and on. Thousands were looking at my darling girl and downloading her recipes. A Facebook Page - Dining With Rosanna was also created and we posted the seasonal recipes there as well. The Facebook Page is still active today.

I became more active in our church, UUCOD in Rancho Mirage. Ken MacLean retired and they now have a new Minister, Rev. Suzanne Marsh. She was so supportive of me and her sermons were excellent. The attendance and membership soared. A stone with Rosanna's name and date is there today, by the entryway among others placed as a remembrance.

I needed to get out of the house, the recent memories were so great. I want to thank those who escorted me out to dinner or other activities in the desert. These were my "Angels". Some were from church. Some were from the community where we lived. One had just celebrated her 100th birthday. She loved to go out, so we made this a regular routine every few weeks. I loved hearing about her life growing up. I thank them all for putting up with my boring conversation. You don't know how much you helped me. I will be forever in your debt.

I was able to continue the Auction Dinners, for both AAUW and our church UUCOD with the help of my "Angel" friends. I helped Rosanna prepare the meat and spices and watched her so often that I felt comfortable enough to be able to do this myself. This went on for several years.

The after meal entertainment was also continued with her piano. The first time I heard the piano played by a guest I had to leave the room, it was too much for me to handle. But eventually I was able to stay and actually enjoyed hearing it being played again.

At age 76, I was still employed, working as an Information Technology contractor for Southern California Edison. Still producing, still solving problems, staying engaged with the new technology being installed. All of this started from a good work ethic, established early in my career. I was laid off in 2011, when the economy went south, but I have stayed in touch with many of my fellow workers.

I decided to sell my home in the desert to move to Modesto to live with my son Geoff. My treasure chest is not empty yet, but is being filled by family activities, Modesto Literary Group and new adventures

As I was packing and sorting through my belongings I came across my "Rosanna Box", the box Rosanna gave me when I mentioned I missed her while I was staying near my work rather than traveling home each night.

These were now her only earthly remains. I immediately sat down, closed my eyes, opened the box and touched her hair. I then lifted the box to my nose to breath in the scent of her perfume. It was heavenly. Was this creepy? Maybe. Do I care? No. For a few minutes I was able to bring her back, sit in her presence, recalling the woman as she was. It was wonderful.

> ....*I love you more each time I smell your hair*
> ......*It fills my senses with something beyond compare*

How many of us, after losing our loved one, haven't gone into their closet and smelled their clothes? (My hand is raised), it gives us a few minutes of love, comfort and peace.

Rosanna's piano used many times for after-meal entertainment, was donated to the Braille Institute in Anaheim CA. They had a children's chorus but needed a piano.

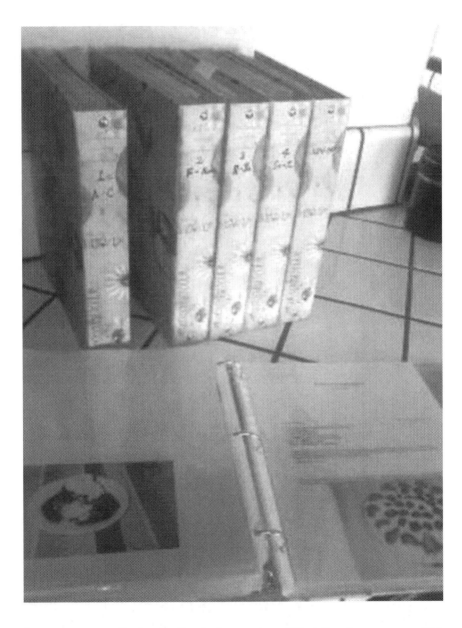

Rosanna was a Gourmet Cook; her recipes filled 7 volumes, over 400 total. Each recipe had a picture of the finished product at the bottom.

Sample Recipe Page.

Each time we entertained she kept a record of the event. This covered a period from October 1998 thru December 2009, 15 volumes. Each guest received the Menu as a souvenir.

For each occasion the pictures included: The menu, picture of the food as delivered to the table, pictures of the table setting, guests and pictures of how they were greeted at the door.

Angels

Angels are God's thoughts to man,
Open your mind be part of the plan;
Let in the goodness for all mankind,
Be there to help or someone unbind.

An angel came to help me today,
She stood there in the doorway;
She asked if I would take her out,
She knew I'd be happy no doubt.

Two angels came to my door today,
An invite to dinner without delay;
We shared a happy friendly meal,
This gave me more time to heal.

An angel came to my side today,
He lifted my spirit but couldn't stay;
He promised to be where I abide,
In time of need on the day I died.

Angels are God's thoughts to man,
Open your mind be part of the plan;
Spread His love in some small way,
Uplift someone you know today.

Erwin's Angels

After Rosanna's passing I was blessed to have many friends who invited me to dinner, help me prepare the auction meals or made sure I got out of the house. This went on during critical times and for several years.

Janet and Dale Webber Paradise Springs next door neighbors invited me to their home for dinner multiple times

Marsha and Cleo Rodriguez Paradise Springs next door neighbors invited me to their home for dinner multiple times

Jean Ogden had her 100th Birthday and loved to go out (She passed away in 2014 at age 101)

Barbara McReal Unitarian Universalist Church of the Desert member. She is also a Docent at the Living Desert.

Rosanna's friend Nancy Moynihan and and neighbor Jane Zaun helped me continue the Auction Diners

Desert Hot Springs neighbors Jane Zaun and Melanie Wilkerson invited me to their home for dinner multiple times

Friend Carmen Covington and her Father

Carmen Covington, like Rosanna, collected Teapots and had books on Tea Etiquette. She is an avid Red Hatter. She was also into sports. We attended boxing matches, movies and watched playoff games while dining. Notice yours truly (eating out a little, huh?) Her Father, US Army Captain George B. Edwards (ret.) a 95 year old WWII Buffalo Soldier, was awarded the Purple Heart. I attended several ceremonies in the Coachella Valley where he was honored. One was at the General George Patton Museum. It was an honor for me to meet him. He passed away in 2016 at age 96.

Erwin's Hero's

Robert Bolton and his wife Josephine on the left, and her daughter Tricia Jane Pintal on the right. Rob works for Southern California Edison where I was a contractor. He and his family were an enormous help to me after Rosanna died.

Henry and Pat Broussard, my Paradise Springs neighbors. Henry helped me with the taxes, putting me in touch with a facilitator to have my mortgage reworked and answered my questions on the sale of my home in Riverside. He was also available anytime to answer the thousands of questions I had on any subject.

There is a place

There is a place once you filled,
That will be empty a long time;
There's a clock that is not ticking
And we'll never hear it chime.

There are people here on earth,
Who will never hear you laugh;
Those who missed your cooking,
Nor will taste your fatted calf.

There is a garden left untilled
Where flowers used to grow;
There's a thimble left unused
Where you used to sit and sew.

There's emptiness in my heart,
That can never be refilled;
There's a piano in the corner,
That has now been stilled.

Rainbows in the making,
Will have a different hue;
A place somewhere in heaven
Has now been filled by you

Chapter 7 Summary
Some comments to help you turn some of these negatives into positives.

1. **Honor your loved one's last wishes**. Although Rosanna wanted no services, I was overwhelmed by those who needed closure. When asked by the church president if I would change my mind, I agreed.

   I was so inspired to see and hear how much she was loved. She also requested that her ashes Be scattered in Oregon. It was easy for me to pick the two places that she loved. She was inspired by what she saw at both of these locations. It gives me comfort to know she is there today still being inspired. Seeing the double rainbow on my return home meant to me "a job well done'. It was special.

2. **Those attending**. Cherish those who attend any service. They are there to support you. Don't obsess over any who cannot attend. They feel worse about it than you do. There are so many factors involved from finances to travel and beyond. Feel the love, they do not need to be present to love you.

3. **Activities and family**. Stay active and in touch with your family and friends. I would even recommend that you increase your activity. You are going to have extra time; stay engaged with people, this interaction will help you move forward. I became more active in our church, UUCOD and in AAUW. Be an angel yourself. Open your mind and I'm sure you will be directed to where you are needed the most.

4. **Be inspired yourself**. Think of something that would make your loved one proud. Creating a Website for Rosanna was my idea, but in a sense it kept her alive as well. Seeing her every day, working on what she loved the most and seeing others interested kept me going. The website was taken down after three years.

5. **Co-Workers**. I will never forget how gracious they were. They were there for me. I am so glad I continued to work as long as possible. I was laid off at age 76. If that didn't happen I would

have worked longer. Stay productive, stay in touch, and stay engaged with others.

6. **Wedding rings**. These are important to me. It is a solemn moment during the wedding and important. Find your comfort level as you move ahead about keeping it on or removing it. I still wear Rosanna's ring.

7. **The Treasure Chest**. It was filled to overflowing by our activities, our pictures and our memories. Continue to add to this chest. All those angels who came helped me add more. I continue to replenish it to this day. This is an endless happy chore, and will keep you busy and inspired.

8. **Traditions**. These are important and I learned this as a child. I believe traditions are the cement that keeps family together. If you have family traditions, I encourage you to keep them going. These are wonderful for the children and grandchildren to see and experience. The passing of your loved one doesn't mean that these have to end, but should inspire you to keep them going.

9. **Angels and Heros**. Recognize and honor your Angels and Heros. We all have them. These are the people that step up and help in your time of need. What would I have done without them? Remember that you too can be someone's angel or hero.

10. **Pay Attention**. Make note of unusual events happening around you. Anything unusual? Did someone enter your life that wasn't there before? I believe things happen for a reason, a higher purpose. Try to recognize these. Even ask others. It might have happened to them as well.

CHAPTER 8

Dreams, Experiences, Incidents and Events

I'm not into dream interpretations. All I can do is share my experience and those of my family members.

Virginia. I did dream of Virginia once, a week after she died. I wrote a poem "There is a River" about that dream. I saw her walking beside the river, looking beautiful. She no longer suffered. I needed to see that, it helped me greatly. That was the only dream I had of her. After her death I would talk to her while out walking.

Rosanna. I never had a dream about Rosanna. I now talk to both Virginia and Rosanna in low whispers while out walking and when I go to bed at night. I think, because of this, I have kept them in my life and there is no need for them to appear in my dreams.

In the following incidents you will see how they both have stayed in my life or have stayed in the lives of other family members. I expect this to continue.

Dream 1

I received a call one morning from my daughter-in-law, Danielle. She said, "I had a dream last night about Virginia" I said, "But you didn't know her. How did you recognize her?" She said "From her pictures" At this point Virginia had been dead 19 years.

The dream: Virginia was seated on the floor surrounded by babies. They were of all races. They were all dressed in white and you could not tell boy from girl. She picked up one baby and showed it to Danielle.

Three to four weeks later Danielle learned from her doctor that she was pregnant. This is startling because, she had been told all her life that she couldn't have children due to internal injuries sustained in an accident. Several months later Danielle had her first child, my first grandchild – Virginia Rosanna Parent. I was 76.

What is also interesting about this dream is that Virginia and I often volunteered to serve in our church nursery. We used to have anywhere from 2 to 6 infants to watch while the parents attended the service. We sometimes ended up walking around with one in each arm to keep them calm. So this scenario didn't surprise me.

Virginia Rosanna Parent

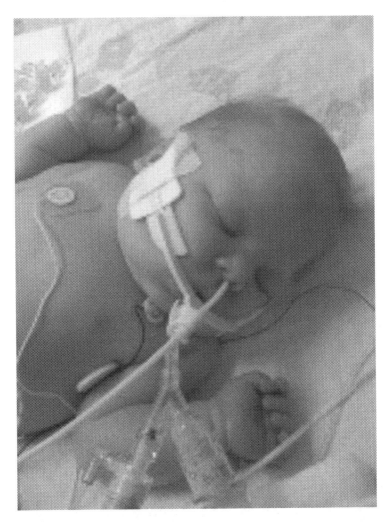

Virginia was born by C-Section and had a seizure during the process at Doctors Hospital in Modesto. She was 2 weeks premature. She weighed 7 Lb.9 oz. She was immediately airlifted to Stanford University Lucille Packard Children's Hospital, NICU (Neo-Natal Intensive Care Unit) and was placed on a Cooling Optimizing Pad to prevent brain damage. The first time I saw her she was shivering. I didn't think she was going to make it. Danielle remained in the Modesto hospital and did not see Virginia again for 4-5 days.

Today Virginia is one of Stanford's NICU success stories. She is a beautiful 4-year old, mildly autistic, but doing great. She loves books.

Animal instincts. Geoff and Danielle have a pet dog named Latte. One evening close to her due date, Danielle was feeling some discomfort. Latte brought her the phone and dropped it in her lap. Danielle put it back on the shelf a little higher than it was before. Again Latte reaches up and gets the phone dropping it in her lap. Danielle said "What do you want me to do? Call Daddy? Will that make you a happy dog?" Geoff was not home and would have been hours before he arrived (he drives a big rig). The third time the dog dropped it in her lap, Danielle called a friend to get her to the hospital. She told me later "That dog saved my life."

****

Dream 2

Fast forward 2 years - another dream by Danielle. The same scenario, Virginia seated on the floor surrounded by babies all dressed in white. This time she picks up a baby, kisses it and hands it to Rosanna. "What? Virginia and Rosanna in the same dream?" "Yes!" "But they didn't know each other!" Again three to four weeks later, Danielle hears from her doctor that she is pregnant. Several months later, my second grand-child was born, Aubree Trudy Parent. I was 79.

Aubree Trudy Parent

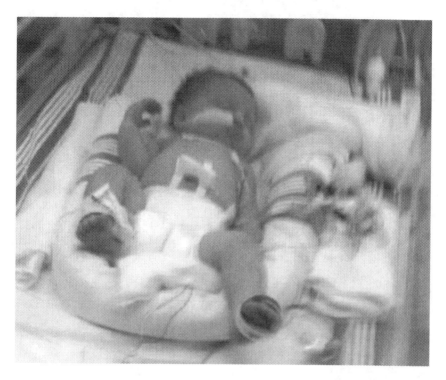

Aubree was born by C-Section, she was 4 weeks premature. She weighed 5 Lb. 13 oz. Her blood pressure was high. She had jaundice and had eating problems.

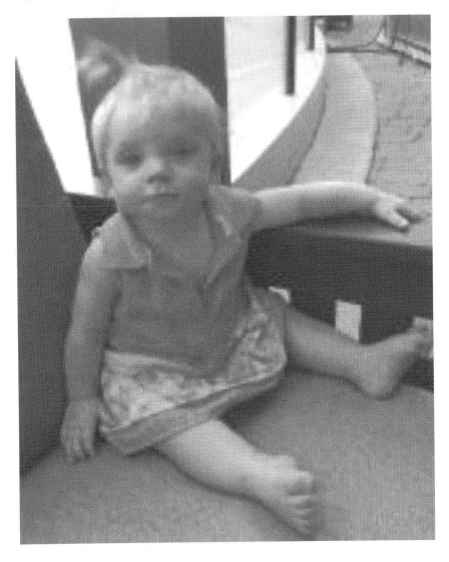

Today Aubree is healthy. She will be two in August 2015. She is active, loves to climb on everything. She is fearless. We are continually taking her off tables, chairs and window sills.

After retiring, I moved in with my son, Geoff. Aubree was born soon after. Since I had three sons, I always wondered what it would be like to have a daughter. Virginia and I had a name selected and even thought of adoption, but it never happened. Here are two verses of a poem I wrote titled "Gabrielle."

> Gabrielle you are the daughter I never had,
> Think what we missed, it seems so sad;
> Nursery floor unwalked, songs unsung,
> To hear you loudly test your lungs.

> Perhaps we will meet in another time,
> I'll polish up my nursery rhymes;
> Perhaps we will meet in another place,
> I can then look into your sweet face.

Each morning while drinking my coffee, I get to sit with Aubree as we watch kid stuff on television. And then, every evening she cuddles up to me and falls asleep. I get to take her upstairs and tuck her into bed. How incredible is that? This wish has been fulfilled.

> .....*Aubree you are the daughter I never had...*
> ....*We meet in another time, I am so glad....*

Dream 3

Another dream by Danielle. The same scenario, Virginia seated on the floor surrounded by babies all dressed in white. She again picks up a baby, kisses it and hands it to Rosanna. This again, is just prior to Danielle's confirmation that she is pregnant. My first grandson, Hunter Alan-Earl Parent, was born in January 2015. I was 80.

Hunter Alan-Earl Parent

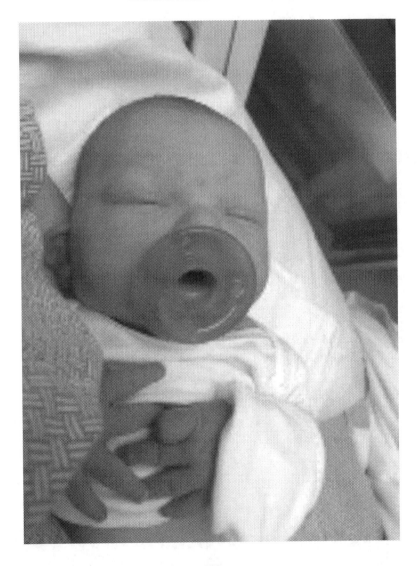

Hunter was born by C-Section full term in Modesto. He weighed 7 Lb.3 oz. He had no health issues.

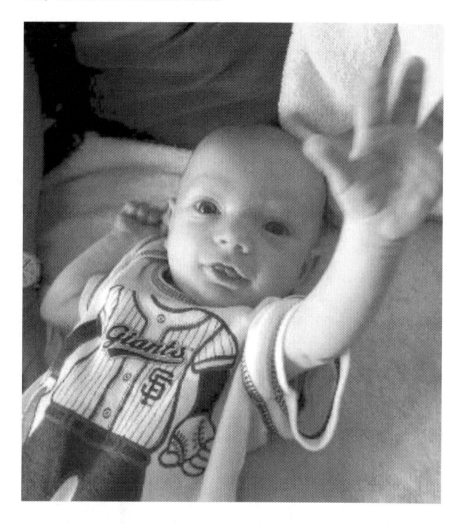

High five dude. Hunter is a happy 3-month old with two big sisters watching over him and, smothering him with kisses.

Back when Virginia was sick, she kept insisting I remarry and not stay single. I didn't want to hear it. I was so concerned about her health. When I met Rosanna, it was so soon and so complete. She met my every need. I suspected then that somehow Virginia was behind the scenes making all this happen. Now hearing that they both were in the same dream, not once but twice, just confirmed my suspicion.

> *Dreams are movies in the theatre of your mind,*
> *Reruns are what we don't want to find*
> *Coming attractions are what we should heed*
> *These are the future and are what we need*

A shopping list item

Rosanna died in September 2010. I was still working. The following December I was preparing to go shopping to get things to take with me. I rented a room close to where I worked. Rain was predicted to begin on Saturday. Rain in the desert is always worrisome because of the flash flooding. In addition, I usually left around 4:30 in the morning on Mondays for my 70 mile drive to work. The worst portion was the drive on the freeway. I had a 2-seater Honda Insite. It was low to the ground. I really hated passing the big rigs because of the spray. I would end up driving blind for a few seconds.

I made a shopping list. My practice was to make the list, then go back over it to determine the quantity and size. After making the list I reviewed it. There in the middle of the list was an item "Window Treatment". I had no clue what that was. I didn't remember writing it down. I walked around the house looking at the windows. I even went outside and did the same.

I was puzzled. Where did that come from and what did it mean? As I sat and thought a few minutes, I remembered a conversation I had with Rosanna during the summer about dreading the coming rainy season. She mentioned something about a product you wipe on the windshield that made the rainwater run right off. Was this thought from her? Did she put this in my little brain and I wrote it down? Why not? I've stayed in touch with her; she knows my issues and concerns. Why wouldn't she want to help?

When I got to the grocery store I immediately went to the automotive section. I stood in front of the shelves that had all of these products. Right in front of me at eye level was a can of windshield treatment and beside it a defogger to wipe on the inside of the window. I bought both. When I arrived home I applied both to the windshield.

It started raining on Saturday. When I left Monday morning it was still raining with lots of water on the roads. The side roads in the desert usually have no street lights, so I had to drive carefully in case of flooding. I reached the freeway and merged into traffic. Immediately there were several big rigs in front of me. I moved to the left to pass the first one. The spray was all over my windshield but it ran right off. I was actually able to see through all the water. What a relief. To this day I believe that it was a heaven-sent message to me from Rosanna, to help me get through this fear.

> *Ideas are like light through a pinhole in a tent*
> *That's why I think they're really heaven sent*

The Mysterious Valentine's Day Card:

After Rosanna passed away, the holiday I dreaded most was Valentine's Day. It was special for us. We usually had a candlelight dinner. I would write a poem and present it to her.

This year, I arrived early to work, around 5:30 AM, before the building was even open. Being in Information Technology I had 24/7 access to my work area.

I used my Security Card to enter the building and the same card to gain access to the suite where my work area was located. When I entered, the only lights on were by the entry way. The cleaning people leave these on when they finish cleaning in the evening. I walked to where I could turn on the area lights. My work station was close by.

I put on my desk lamp, turned on my PC and emptied my briefcase. I then walked to start the coffee maker and to turn on three large copier/printers nearby. It takes them awhile to warm up.

When I returned to my desk there was a card that wasn't there when I arrived. The door is heavy and makes a loud noise when it closes and locks and I didn't hear anyone come in or go out. I opened and read the card. I was astonished. I then walked around to see who had come in. I retraced my steps back to where I had been. No overhead lights were on nor any desk lamps. I yelled out to anyone who was there. I walked around the entire office area. I was alone. I then returned to my desk and read the card again.

Printed on the front –
   "May today bring you blessing from above"

Printed inside left –
   A quote from the Bible "Love never fails" (I Corinthians 13:8, KJV)

Printed inside right –
   "Peace, joy, happiness
   The perfect gifts of love!
   Happy Valentine's Day"

Hand written on the card –
   "Isn't it wonderful to know that someone who loves you is in Heaven looking down on you."
The card was unsigned.

I sat there awhile and sobbed. Somehow my darling girl had found a way to cross all the barriers that separated us to reach me on our special day. Had some "earth angel" delivered this card to me? Getting through all the security to reach me? I'm convinced the answer is "Yes."

(Valentine's Day for us was special)

Valentine's Day 1994

My love for you grows more each day,
The way you smile, the things you say;
The hours together are still too few,
My happiest hours are those with you.

My love for you grows more each week,
You touch my hand, you kiss my cheek;
The days together are fewer still,
My happiest days are those you fill.

My love grows more as months go by,
The gourmet meals, the clothes you buy;
My days are filled with happiness,
My soul fulfilled by your caress.

My love for you grows more each year,
The fireplace logs, when you are near;
You are my love in every way,
Not just once on Valentine's Day.

(Every day should be special)

A paranormal event – A Night Visitor

One evening when I was in bed and after talking to both Virginia and Rosanna, I felt someone sit on the bed. The room was dark so I couldn't see. The side of the bed sagged and the covers pulled away from my neck. Then someone reached out and touched my head. I laid there for a few moments hardly breathing. Then, I moved my hand down under the covers to where they were sitting. Nothing was there.

To this day it is a mystery. Was it Virginia? Was it Rosanna? I think I would have sensed if it was either one. It was not a cold and frightening event, but rather warm and loving. It has not happened since.

"…an angel touched him…" (A Bible quote I Kings 19:7 – KJV)

> *Angels on the left, angels on the right,*
> *Angels with me throughout the night;*
> *Bringing me peace until morning light,*
> *Or an angel myself, I'll take flight.*

*(To lose both Virginia and Rosanna on a Sunday in
September is more than I could ever imagine)*

Sundays in September

Sundays in September will never be the same,
To lose a loved one is more than I can bear:
Remember the Sabbath Day I will, I will,
But to lose them both like this must be rare.

To lose Virginia mother of my children,
Her singing voice will never be heard again;
Remember the Sabbath Day I will, I will,
My tears are mixed with the falling rain.

To lose Rosanna with her beautiful smile,
Her presence in my life never felt again;
Remember the Sabbath Day I will, I will,
It's hard to forget and I relive the pain.

Sundays in September will never be the same,
To lose a loved one is more than I can bear:
Remember the Sabbath Day I will, I will,
But to lose them both just doesn't seem fair.

Final Thoughts

Here are my final comments.

I believe that when you are in your darkest hour, in the deepest pit of despair, this is when you are closest to God. Reach out and touch His loving face. Let Him fill your mind with inspiration, ideas and good thoughts. Let Him fill your heart with love, compassion and forgiveness. Let Him fill your soul with completeness, satisfaction and fullness.

When my end is near I will take my "Rosanna box," her only earthly remains. I will close my eyes and I will touch her hair and lift it to my nose to smell her perfume. I will recall listening to Rosanna play Beethoven's "Fur Elise" on her Ivory Piano and then I will enter heaven.

I have two wonderful women waiting there for me. Heck I might even skip there.

Chapter 8 Summary

Some comments to help you turn some of these negatives into positives.

1. **Your loved one**. Stay connected to your loved one. Because they are out of sight doesn't mean they are not with you in some way. Keep your loved one in your life by talking to them. Stay connected forever. You may not get a verbal response, but I feel you will see evidence of this yourself or you will hear from other family members.

2. **Expect the unexpected**. Who knows how the response will come. Don't be too quick to dismiss an event. Share it with others. Perhaps they had an event as well, but didn't relate it to your loved one.

3. **Family**. Stay close to them. I'm so grateful that I stayed in touch with my sons. I encourage everyone to do the same. If you have lost touch or there was an incident that separated you – reconnect with them. There is no need for this to go on forever. With all the social media connections available it is getting easier. If you need assistance ask a friend to help with this effort..

   My mother came to live with Virginia and me after my father passed away. During this time she received a letter from a sister that she had not heard from in over 45 years. When my mother and father married they were disowned by their families, because they had different religious beliefs. I never met many of my cousins, aunts and uncles. Her sister was asking, "How many children did you have? Where are they now?" How sad. My mother talked often of a younger brother, Vincent. She never saw him again. Don't let something like this stand in the way of your reaching out to others. People do and say stupid things. Man-up, woman-up or stand-up to be sure you connect again. You will be glad that you did.

4. **Dreams.** They come for a reason. Not always by you, but like in my case, by others. It was comforting for me to hear that both Virginia and Rosanna appeared in the same dream. Rosanna

knew Danielle, but Virginia never met her. Don't believe that this can't happen to you or your loved one.

5. **Treasure Chest**. Don't forget to continue to add to the Treasure Chest. Memories, pictures of life events. Fill it to overflowing.

6. **Pets.** Latte, Danielle's dog was sensing something. This was her first child, so it's not something that Latte had experienced before. The dog's actions prompted her to get to the hospital. We need to pay attention to animals, they know far more than we give them credit for.

7. **Facebook**. Please check in on my Facebook Page "Author Erwin Parent" I would like to get feedback on this book. What inspiration did you receive? Have you had any similar experiences? I would like to keep everyone informed and will post information on any upcoming events.

** THE END **

EPILOGUE

While writing this book I discovered something I didn't expect. The further I went back in memory, specially going through the painful events, the sharper my memory became.

I would encourage anyone with Alzheimer's to begin writing a Memoir. Start with a single page, pictures help. If there are painful periods have someone help you get through this.

At age 80, I was able to go back to when I was 4 or 5 and my Mother took my sister and I on a bus and trolley to several events. When I went back to the event when I met Virginia, I realized I had never thanked my sister Cathy for introducing us. She is 83 and in a nursing home. She is mentally okay, but just lost her husband Linwood. I hurriedly got a thank you note to one of her daughters to take to her and read it. The response was so satisfying and I am so grateful that I was able to correct that.

I am documenting all of this separately, perhaps I can write something to share with other families and especially Alzheimer care-givers.

ABOUT THE AUTHOR

Erwin Alan Parent

Erwin is new to the literary world, recently attending meetings with the Modesto Literary Group in Modesto CA. This is his first published book.

Erwin was born in Haverhill MA on November 18, 1934. He attended schools in Somerville, MA graduating from Somerville High School in 1953.

He enlisted in the U.S. Army immediately after to avoid the Draft for the Korean conflict, and was discharged in 1956 after serving 3 years. Two of the years were spent in France. While in the military he gained experience using IBM equipment, this became his vocation and launched a near-60 year career in Information Technology.

He attended Northeastern University in Boston MA for a brief period concentrating on accounting and job related computer courses.

He relocated to Los Angeles CA in 1971.

He credits his mother and father for instilling a good work ethic. On his last day at work, as an Information Technology Consultant at Southern California Edison, he was 76. During that 60 year period of employment there were very few gaps.

He thanks his parents also for early involvement in religion. He was brought up as a Christian Scientist and later served in many of their churches in Boston area and California. He continues to read the Bible every day. He credits this for giving him a good moral compass and the day-to-day inspiration which he hopes shows in his writings. He currently has four books of poetry underway.

Printed in the United States
By Bookmasters